Beading
Inspiration
How to use COLOR in jewelry design

Printed in the United States of America

11 10 09 08 07   1 2 3 4 5

Publisher's Cataloging-In-Publication Data
(Prepared by The Donohue Group, Inc.)

Beading inspiration : how to use color in jewelry design.

    p. : col. ill. ; cm.

  ISBN: 978-0-87116-246-5

1. Beadwork--Handbooks, manuals, etc. 2. Beads--Handbooks, manuals, etc. 3. Jewelry making--Handbooks, manuals, etc. 4. Color in design. I. Title: Bead&Button magazine.

TT860 .B433 2007
745.594/2

All projects have appeared previously in *Beading Basics: Color*, a special issue from *Bead&Button* and *BeadStyle* magazines, except those by Helene Tsigistras on pages 38, 44, 64, 72, 83, and 88. Special thanks to Ms. Tsigistras and the talented staffs of both magazines for their help in making this publication possible.

Introduction

Color is an essential element of jewelry design, but many beaders and jewelry designers struggle to find color combinations that work. Choosing the right hues and proportions can be intimidating, but with a little color knowledge and an eye for inspiration, it becomes very easy. *Beading Inspiration: How to use COLOR in jewelry design* will show you the basics of working with color and teach you to find the right hues for every project by using four proven sources of inspiration: the color wheel, nature, fabric, and decorative art.

Color trends change over time, but using a few basic guidelines makes it easy to find colors that work together for harmony or contrast. A rudimentary understanding of color relationships is easy to achieve with a basic color wheel. You may already know some of the basics: red, yellow, and blue are primary colors; combined they create secondary colors (red + yellow = orange, yellow + blue = green, and blue + red = violet). Mixing these six colors creates tertiary colors, like red orange or indigo (blue violet).

We've organized this book on a spectrum to show a range of color possibilities using every hue in the rainbow. In addition to the traditional colors of the rainbow, we've also created projects featuring colors that don't appear on the typical spectrum: brown, black and white, and metallics. Color itself can be wonderful inspiration, and when you understand the relationship between colors, the color wheel becomes a perfect tool for making beautiful jewelry.

Inspiration and ideas abound in the world around you. Look outside and you'll see that nature has color combinations that range from neutral to shocking, and these combinations are a great source for beading ideas. Fabric is another excellent source of inspiration. Coordinating beads to fabric is a natural for anyone who has matched a necklace to an outfit. Fabric designers know their colors, and finding a fabric that strikes your fancy can make it easy to select bead colors to match your taste. For more winning color combinations, look around your home, or in stores and magazines for decorative art items. The translucent blues of a glass vase or the mottled golds of a decorative plate may be the perfect palette for creating a piece of jewelry you'll love to wear.

Creating beautiful, colorful jewelry is easy. All you need is the right inspiration and a few basic techniques. To get started, look at our inspiration guide on page 6 for great color ideas. If you're new to beading, learn the basics on page 8. Then turn the page for a colorful range of beautiful jewelry projects that will teach you to make color work for you.

Contents

Inspiration

Use these four sources as inspiration for your own colorful jewelry designs

COLOR WHEEL

Of all the tools available for making beautiful jewelry, a good color wheel is one of the most important. A color wheel is a great tool for developing color schemes based on color relationships such as these:

• **analogous colors** – three or four adjacent colors on the color wheel, such as yellow, yellow orange, and orange
• **complementary colors** – colors directly opposite each other on the color wheel, such as red and green
• **split complementary colors** – any color plus the colors on each side of its complement, such as red, green blue, and yellow green
• **triad** – three colors equally spaced on the color wheel, such as red, yellow, and blue
• **tetrad** – any two colors and their complements, such as red, green, indigo, and orange yellow
• **monochromatic** – different values of the same color, such as black, gray, and white

NATURE

Here's a truism we're eager to pass along: When it comes to color combinations, nature is always right. From butterfly wings to flowers to seashells, nature's palette can guide color choices with great success. Look closely, and you'll find ample inspiration. Take time to linger over the fascinating objects of the natural world and look for details such as texture or iridescence. Consider proportion and scale. Observe the item when it is in motion or at rest. Whether you enjoy making the simplest styles of jewelry or the most complex, nature's lessons are among the most valuable to learn.

FABRIC

If you love the colors in a piece of fabric, chances are you'll love the way those colors look in jewelry, too. Following a few basic guidelines can make your designs more successful. First, keep the proportions of color in line with what is in fabric. Although this tip can be ignored over time, it provides a good starting point for your designs. Second, experiment with combining bead colors in a range of values that mimic the lighter or darker hues found throughout a fabric's design. Combining values adds interest to your work. Third, no matter how elaborate the fabric, work with a reasonable number of bead colors. The reward will be a lovely, harmonious, and manageable piece.

DECORATIVE ARTS

Look around and consider the decorative objects in your surroundings. What catches your eye – the bold color combinations of a contemporary decanter, the unusual hues of an antique quilt, a set of brightly colored coasters, or the fine art painting hanging on your wall?

One of the easiest and most successful ways to develop a palette for a piece of jewelry is to start with the colors in an item you enjoy. But don't stop there. Always consider texture, finish, shape, and opacity when making beading decisions.

Basics

Plain loop

1 Trim the wire or head pin ⅜ in. (1cm) above the top bead. Make a right-angle bend close to the bead.

2 Grab the wire's tip with roundnose pliers. The tip of the wire should be flush with the pliers. Roll the wire to form a half circle. Release the wire.

3 Reposition the pliers in the loop and continue rolling.

4 The finished loop should form a centered circle above the bead.

Wrapped loop

1 Make sure you have at least 1¼ in. (3.2cm) of wire above the bead. With the tip of your chainnose pliers, grasp the wire directly above the bead. Bend the wire (above the pliers) into a right angle.

2 Using roundnose pliers, position the jaws in the bend.

3 Bring the wire over the top jaw of the roundnose pliers.

4 Reposition the pliers' lower jaw snugly into the loop. Curve the wire downward around the bottom of the roundnose pliers. This is the first half of a wrapped loop.

5 Position the chainnose pliers' jaws across the loop.

6 Wrap the wire around the wire stem, covering the stem between the loop and the top bead. Trim the excess wire and press the cut end close to the wraps with chainnose pliers.

Opening and closing jump rings

1 Hold the loop or jump ring with two pairs of chainnose pliers or chainnose and roundnose pliers, as shown.

2 To open the loop or jump ring, bring one pair of pliers toward you and push the other pair away. String materials on the open loop or jump ring. Reverse the steps to close the open loop or jump ring.

Wrapped loop over a top-drilled bead

  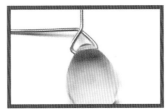 

1 Center a top-drilled bead on a 3-in. (7.6cm) piece of wire. Bend each wire upward to form a squared-off "U" shape.

2 Cross the wires into an "X" above the bead.

3 Using chainnose pliers, make a small bend in each wire so the ends form a right angle.

4 Wrap the horizontal wire around the vertical wire as in a wrapped loop. Trim the excess wire.

Overhand knot

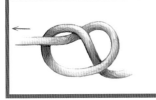

Make a loop and pass the working end through it. Pull the ends to tighten the knot.

Square knot

1 Cross the right-hand cord over the left-hand cord, and then bring it under the left-hand cord from back to front. Pull it up in front so both ends are facing upward.

2 Cross right over left, forming a loop, and go through the loop, again from back to front. Pull the ends to tighten the knot.

Surgeon's knot

Cross the left end over the right end and go through the loop. Pull the ends to tighten. Cross the right end over the left end and go through the loop. Go through again. Pull the ends to tighten.

Half-hitch knot

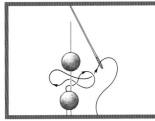

Come out a bead and form a loop perpendicular to the thread between beads. Bring the needle under the thread away from the loop. Then go back over the thread and through the loop. Pull gently so the knot doesn't tighten prematurely.

Flattened crimp

1 Hold the crimp using the tip of your chainnose pliers. Squeeze the pliers firmly to flatten the crimp.

2 Tug the wire to make sure the crimp has a solid grip. If the wire slides, remove the crimp and repeat the steps with a new crimp.

Crimp covers

Cup the crimp cover around the crimped crimp bead and gently close with chainnose pliers or the notch near the tip of your crimping pliers.

Folded crimp

1 Position the crimp bead in the notch closest to the crimping pliers' handle.

2 Separate the wires and firmly squeeze the crimp.

3 Move the crimp into the notch at the pliers' tip and hold the crimp as shown. Squeeze the crimp bead, folding it in half at the indentation.

4 Test that the folded crimp is secure.

Gentle wire handling lends professional results to crystal rings.

Red

Make dazzling rings using wire wraps to connect faceted crystals

by Cheryl Phelan

Two shades of red, one dark and one light, create a rich background for a lone accent of yellow or violet – colors taken from a swatch of quilting fabric. Notice how the accent colors add life to the reds, even when used in small quantities. But color is not the only element this fabric inspires. To capture the mosaic-like surface of the fabric, choose sparkling, faceted briolettes.

inspiration fabric

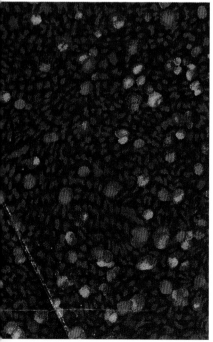

materials

one ring
- 6mm round Swarovski crystal
- 6–8 11 x 5mm briolettes
- 6 4mm round Swarovski crystals
- 20 in. (51cm) 22-gauge sterling silver wire
- 8 in. (20cm) 28-gauge craft wire, silver
- beading cord, .006
- G-S Hypo cement
- twisted-wire needles
- chainnose pliers
- flatnose pliers (optional)
- diagonal wire cutters
- ring mandrel or other ring-sized cylinder
- metal file

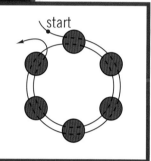
start

1 Using a twisted-wire needle and 8 in. (20cm) of beading cord, pick up six 4mm round crystals and sew through them again in the same direction, leaving a 3-in. (7.6cm) tail.

2 Tie the tail and working thread together with a square knot (see Basics, p. 8), and glue the knot. Sew through the next bead in the ring and pull the knot into the bead.

3 Tie the working cord around the cord between beads with a half-hitch knot (Basics), and sew through the next bead. Repeat twice, then trim the cord. Repeat with the cord's tail end.

4 String six to eight briolettes on an 8-in. piece of 28-gauge wire. Bend the beads into a circle, leaving a 3-in. tail on one end. Twist the long wire and the tail together to hold the beads in place.

5 Bring the long wire over the briolette to the right, over the wire in the circle, and down behind the briolettes.

6 Bring the wire up to the front through the center of the circle.

7 Wrap the wire around the circle again.

8 Repeat steps 5–7 with each briolette to lock them all in place. Hold the briolettes with your nondominant hand as you wrap, and avoid wrapping tight enough to break a bead.

9 Trim the wires and tuck them down between the briolettes with your pliers.

10 Turn the briolettes over. Use the back of the cluster as the top surface of the petals.

11 Center a 6mm round crystal on the 22-gauge wire. Use chainnose pliers to bend the wire as shown in the photo. Don't bend the wire against the crystal or the crystal may crack.

12 To assemble the flower, string the 4mm crystals and the briolettes onto the wire ends and slide them against the 6mm crystal. Separate the wires behind the briolettes.

13 Hold the flower in place on a ring mandrel or other cylinder. Make sure the band is slightly larger than the diameter of your finger. Wrap each end of the wire around the mandrel two times.

14 Working with one end at a time, coil the wire under the flower with two or more wraps. These support the briolette petals. Make an additional wrap or two if needed, then remove the ring from the mandrel.

15 Wrap one wire around the band three to four times. Use flatnose pliers to hold the band wires together as you wrap. Trim the wire on the inside of the band, pinch the end against the band with pliers, and file the end. Repeat on the other side.

16 Slide the ring back on the mandrel to reshape the band.

Red

Beads intertwine gracefully in a five-strand necklace

by Diane Jolie

inspiration
decorative art

Mixing reds can be tricky, but using the striking mix of colors found in this dramatic glass vase for inspiration makes it easy. In addition to reds, which can easily overpower most other colors, try using muted purples – red's neighbor on the color wheel – to temper its force. Sparks of gold from interspersed seed beads brighten the overall effect.

materials

necklace 17 in. (43cm)
- focal bead (Eclectica, 262-641-0910)
- 120 3 x 4mm drops, red
- 2 4mm round beads
- 3mm fire-polished beads
  120 purple
  120 red
- seed beads
  4g size 6º, 1–2 colors
  2g size 11º, gold
- 2 medium cones
- toggle clasp
- flexible beading wire, .014
- 10-in. (25cm) 20-gauge wire
- 10 crimp beads
- chainnose pliers
- roundnose pliers
- crimping pliers (optional)
- diagonal wire cutters

1 Determine the finished length of your necklace (this one is 17 in./43cm), add 6 in. (15cm), and cut five pieces of flexible beading wire to that length. Center the focal bead on one piece of wire.

2 String 6º seed beads on each end until you are 1 in. (2.5cm) short of the desired length. Make sure the total number of 6ºs is divisible by four. String an 11º, a crimp bead, and an 11º on each end. Tape the ends.

3 Make a wrapped loop (see Basics, p. 8) on one end of a 5-in. (13cm) piece of 20-gauge wire. Remove the tape from one end and string the wrapped loop. Go back through the 11º, the crimp bead, the 11º, and three 6ºs. Crimp the crimp bead (Basics) and trim the tail.

4 To start the second strand, string an 11º, a crimp bead, and an 11º. Go through the wrapped loop made in step 3 and back through the 11º, the crimp bead, and the 11º. Crimp the crimp bead and trim the tail.

5 Go through the first 6º on the finished strand. String an 11º, a purple fire-polished bead, a drop bead, a purple bead, and an 11º. Skip three 6ºs on the finished strand and go through the fourth 6º.

6 Repeat this pattern until you reach the focal bead. Then go through the focal bead and continue to the other end. As you approach the end of this and subsequent strands, adjust your final bead count so you always exit the last 6º. String an 11º, a crimp bead, and an 11º. Tape the end.

7 Start the third strand as in step 5. Then string one 11º and a red fire-polished bead. Go through the second 6º on the first strand. String a red, an 11º, a drop, an 11º, and a red. Skip three 6ºs on the finished strand and go through the fourth 6º as before. Work in this pattern and end as in step 6.

8 Start the fourth strand as in step 5. String two 11ºs, a purple, and an 11º. Go through the third 6º. String an 11º, a purple, a drop, a purple, and an 11º. Skip three 6ºs on the finished strand and go through the fourth 6º as before. Work in this pattern and end as in step 6.

editor's tip

To keep this necklace flexible, make sure you maintain a consistent tension among all five strands and allow some ease in each strand before you crimp it.

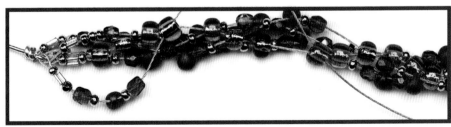

9 Start the fifth strand as in step 5. String a red, an 11º, a drop, an 11º, and a red. Go through the fourth 6º. String the pattern again, skip three 6ºs on the finished strand, and go through the fourth 6º as before. Work in this pattern and end as in step 6.

10 Make a wrapped loop on the end of a 5-in. piece of 20-gauge wire. Using one strand of the necklace at a time, untape the ends, string the wrapped loop, and go back through the 11º, the crimp bead, the 11º and the last few beads on the strand. Repeat with all the other strands, snug up the beads, and crimp the crimp beads.

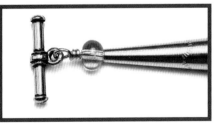

11 String a cone on the wire at one end of the strands and pull the strands into the cone. String a round bead on the wire and make the first half of a wrapped loop. Slide the clasp into the loop, then finish the wraps. Repeat at the other end of the necklace.

This necklace has the added detail of crystals cascading from its clasp

Red
Orange

An array of fiery crystals dangles from tiers of chain

by Anna Elizabeth Draeger

A crystal necklace in a striking palette of red-to-gold crystals evokes the hot colors of autumn mums. By centering the darkest red and flanking it with progressively lighter shades of red, orange, and gold, the colors blend seamlessly. This gradient effect is intensified by its repetition on three strands. The earrings, long and dramatic, capture the same fiery appeal.

materials

both projects
- chainnose pliers
- roundnose pliers
- diagonal wire cutters

necklace 17 in. (43cm)
- Swarovski crystals
  5 5mm bicones, siam
  22 4mm rounds, light siam
  20 4mm bicones, hyacinth
  20 4mm bicones, fire opal
  28 4mm bicones, sun
- lobster claw clasp
- 45 in. (1.1m) 3.6mm long-and-short diamond chain (riogrande.com)
- 95 1 in. (2.5cm) 24-gauge head pins
- 6 6mm jump rings

earrings
- Swarovski crystals, **12** each of the following:
  5mm bicones, siam
  4mm round, light siam
  4mm bicones, hyacinth
  4mm bicones, fire opal
  4mm bicones, sun
- 5½ in. (14cm) 2mm cable chain
- 60 1 in. (2.5cm) 24-gauge head pins
- 2 3mm jump ring
- pair post earring findings with loop

1 **necklace** • String a crystal on a head pin. Make a plain loop (see Basics, p. 8) above the crystal. Repeat with all the remaining crystals.

2 Cut the chain into pieces as follows: three 1 in. (2.5cm), four 3½ in. (8.9cm), one 6 in. (15cm), one 7 in. (18cm), one 8 in. (20cm).

3 Open a jump ring (Basics) and attach the clasp to a 1-in. chain. Close the jump ring.

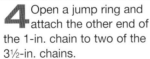

4 Open a jump ring and attach the other end of the 1-in. chain to two of the 3½-in. chains.

5 Open a jump ring and connect the two 3½ in. chains to the 6-in., 7-in., and 8-in. chains. Connect the chains to finish the other end of the necklace the same way as the first, being careful not to cross the chains. Then attach another 1-in. chain to the last jump ring.

inspiration nature

6 To attach the dangles, find the two large center links on the longest chain. Attach two siam-colored dangles to each link. Working from the center toward one end, attach two dangles to each large link in the following color combinations: siam and light siam, two light siam, two light siam, two hyacinth, two hyacinth, hyacinth and fire opal, two fire opal, two fire opal, two sun, two sun. To finish this end, attach one sun dangle to each of the next five large links. Repeat on the other side of the center dangles.

7 Attach a siam dangle to the center large link of the middle chain. Working from the center toward one end, add one dangle per large link as follows: siam, light siam, light siam, hyacinth, hyacinth, fire opal, fire opal, sun, sun. Repeat on the other side of the center dangle.

8 Attach a siam dangle to the center large link of the shortest chain. Working from the center toward one end, add one dangle per large link as follows: siam, light siam, light siam, hyacinth, fire opal, sun. Repeat on other side of the center dangle.

9 To embellish the 1-in. chain at the back of the necklace, attach three siam dangles to the end link. Then attach the remaining colors to subsequent links, working from the darkest to lightest and adding two of each color on each side of each link.

1 **earrings •** Make dangles as in step 1 of the necklace. Cut a 1-in. (2.5cm) and a 1½-in. (3.8cm) piece of chain. Use jump rings to attach the 1-in. chain to the ball of the earring finding and the 1½-in. chain to the ear nut.

2 Attach three siam-colored dangles to the end link of the 1½-in. chain. Then work as follows, attaching one dangle of each pair to each side of each chain link: two light siam, light siam and hyacinth, two hyacinth, two fire opal, fire opal and sun, two sun. Repeat on the 1-in. chain. Make a second earring to match the first.

Carnelian gemstones take center stage in a necklace, bracelet, and earrings trio

by Linda Augsburg

A repeating pattern of carnelians and crystals adds a formal touch to an easy jewelry ensemble.

Red Orange

With the red-orange of carnelian beads as a starting point, you may first have considered using its complement, blue-green, for a high-contrast color scheme. Equally bold, but definitely unexpected, is a color wheel relationship called a tertiary basic triad – tertiary because each color is a combination of primary and secondary colors, and a basic triad because red-orange, blue-violet, and yellow-green are evenly spaced on the color wheel.

inspiration color wheel

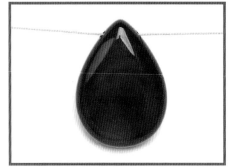

1 **necklace •** Determine the finished length of your necklace, (this one is 17 in./43cm), add 6 in. (15cm), and cut a piece of beading wire to that length.

2 Center the teardrop pendant on the wire.

4 On one end, string a gold-filled bead, a crimp bead, a gold-filled bead, and a lobster claw clasp. String the same sequence on the other end, substituting a soldered jump ring for the clasp. Check the fit, and add or remove beads from each end if necessary. Crimp the crimp beads (see Basics, p. 8) and trim the excess wire.

3 On each side of the pendant, string a 2mm carnelian, a 4mm crystal, a 2mm, a spacer, an 8mm carnelian, a spacer, a 2mm, a 6mm crystal, a 2mm, a spacer, an 8mm, and a spacer. Repeat this pattern on each end until the necklace is 1 in. (2.5cm) short of the desired length.

1 **earrings •** Cut a 10-in. (25cm) piece of beading wire. String a spacer, an 8mm carnelian, a spacer, a 6mm crystal, a spacer, an 8mm, a spacer, a 4mm crystal, a spacer, an 8mm, a spacer, a 6mm, a spacer, an 8mm, and a spacer. Center these beads on the wire.

2 On each end, string a 3mm crystal, three 2mm carnelians, a 3mm, three 2mm, a 3mm, and a 2mm.

3 String an 8mm and a crimp bead over both ends. Bring both ends around the earring's loop and back through the last beads strung. Crimp the crimp bead and trim the excess wire. Make a second earring to match the first.

materials

necklace 17 in. (43cm)
- 18 x 25mm teardrop pendant
- 22 8mm round carnelian beads
- 10 6mm round crystals, tanzanite
- 12 4mm round crystals, olivine AB
- 44 2mm round carnelian beads
- 44 4mm vermeil daisy spacers
- 4 2.5mm round gold-filled beads
- lobster claw clasp and soldered jump ring
- flexible beading wire, .012
- 2 crimp beads
- chainnose or crimping pliers
- diagonal wire cutters

earrings
- 10 8mm round carnelian beads
- 4 6mm round crystals, tanzanite
- 2 4mm round crystals, olivine AB
- 12 3mm bicone crystals, olivine AB
- 28 2mm round carnelian beads
- 16 4mm vermeil daisy spacers
- flexible beading wire, .012
- 2 crimp beads
- pair of earring findings
- chainnose or crimping pliers
- diagonal wire cutters

bracelet 8 in. (20cm)
- 16-in. (41cm) strand or 35 8mm round carnelian beads
- 17 6mm round crystals, tanzanite
- 17 4mm crystals, olivine AB
- 72 4mm vermeil daisy spacers
- 6 2.5mm round gold-filled beads
- flexible beading wire, .012
- 6 crimp beads
- three-strand box clasp
- chainnose or crimping pliers
- diagonal wire cutters

1 bracelet • Determine the finished length of your bracelet, (this one is 8 in./20cm), add 5 in. (13cm), and cut three pieces of beading wire to that length. Tape one end of each wire.

2 On the bottom strand, string a spacer, an 8mm carnelian, a spacer, a 6mm crystal, a spacer, an 8mm, a spacer, and a 4mm crystal. Repeat until the strand is 1 in. (2.5cm) short of the desired length. Tape the end.

3 On the middle strand, string a spacer, a 4mm, a spacer, an 8mm, a spacer, a 6mm, a spacer, and an 8mm. Repeat until the strand is 1 in. (2.5cm) short of the desired length. Tape the end.

4 On the top strand, string a spacer, an 8mm, a spacer, a 4mm, a spacer, an 8mm, a spacer, and a 6mm. Repeat until the strand is 1 in. (2.5cm) short of the desired length. Tape the end.

5 Remove the tape on the middle strand. String a crimp bead, a gold-filled bead, and the center loop on the clasp to each respective end. Repeat with the bottom and top strands. Close the clasp to allow some ease on each strand. Check the fit, and add or remove beads if necessary. Crimp the crimp beads and trim the excess wire.

Orange

Use a classic wire-wrapping technique to make vibrant earrings

by Debbie Nishihara

When you take your cue from colors sitting next to each other on the color wheel, your reward will be jewelry in gradations of harmonious colors. Here, hot-colored crystals in oranges and yellows surround a golden bicone. The solar effect is intensified by using larger crystals to create a luminous ring around the edge.

materials

earrings
- Swarovski bicone crystals
  2 5mm, light topaz or citrine
  10 4mm, fire opal
  4 4mm, sun
  4 4mm, hyacinth
  12 3mm, hyacinth
- 5g size 11º seed beads, orange
- 28-gauge craft wire, gold
- pair of earring wires
- T-pin
- chainnose pliers
- diagonal wire cutters

These brilliant disks employ a centuries-old technique used to make three-dimensional beaded flowers. By changing the bead counts, a disk can be elongated into an oval, much like the traditional shape of a petal or leaf.

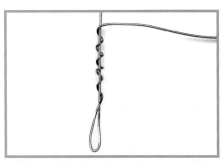

1 Cut a 2-ft. (61cm) length of wire. Make a small loop at one end, leaving a 6-in. (15cm) tail. Wrap the wire's long end (the working wire) around the tail so the loop and the wraps equal 1 in. (2.5cm). Do not cut the wire.

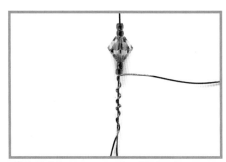

2 Holding your work with the loop at the bottom, string two 11º seed beads, a 5mm bicone crystal, and two 11ºs on the tail. These are the only beads strung on the tail end.

3 String nine 11ºs on the working wire.

4 Curve the working wire around the crystal. Wrap it around the tail directly above the top two 11°s, with the wrap going over the tail.

5 String ten 11°s, curve the wire around the crystal, and wrap it around the tail close to the beads. Continue adding rows of 11°s, increasing the count by one or more beads in each row as necessary, until there are four rows on each side of the crystal. Straighten the tail after every wrap.

6 For the outer row, string six 11°s, a 3mm bicone, three 11°s, a 3mm bicone, an 11°, a 3mm bicone, a 4mm hyacinth bicone, two 4mm fire opal bicones, and a 4mm sun bicone. Wrap the working wire around the tail as before. Then string this sequence in reverse to finish the other side.

7 Wrap the working wire around the loop end of the tail close to the beads, and cut the working wire about ¼ in. (6mm) from the last wrap. Press the cut end against the beads.

8 Fold the straight end of the tail to the back of the work and cut it.

9 Turn your work so the loop is at the top. Pinch the loop closed tightly with chainnose pliers.

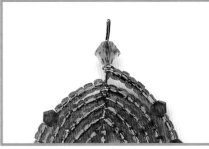

10 String a fire opal bicone over the closed loop.

11 Open the loop above the bicone by inserting a T-pin.

12 Use chainnose pliers to twist the loop so the opening faces front to back.

13 Open the loop on an earring wire (see Basics, p. 8) and attach the earring. Make a second earring to match the first.

inspiration color wheel

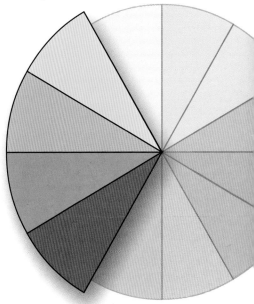

Orange

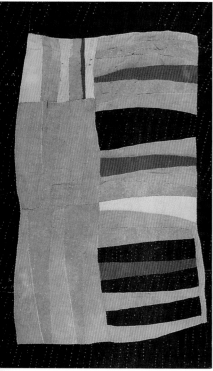

The Gee's Bend quilt photo is from the collection of the Tinwood Alliance. Photo by Steve Pitkin.

Create two bracelets using one color palette in different proportions

by Cathy Jakicic

Because of its high intensity, bright orange is at its most forceful when teamed up with black, but adding other colors to the mix tones down the drama. This quilt, one of the remarkable pieces from the Gee's Bend collection, inspired this pairing of red-orange carnelian stones with melon and amber seed beads and peach pearls. Don't hesitate to add green – take the plunge, and you'll achieve an unusual and energetic color scheme.

editor's tip
Be sure to choose beads, especially pearls, with holes large enough to string on memory wire.

1 **two-strand bracelet** • Determine the finished length of your bracelet (this one is 7 in./18cm), add 5 in. (13cm), and cut two pieces of beading wire to that length. On one strand, string a crimp bead, an 8° seed bead, and the clasp. Go back through the beads and tighten the wire. Crimp the crimp bead (see Basics, p. 8) and trim the excess wire.

4 Remove the tape from the first strand and string a crimp bead, an 8°, and a soldered jump ring. Go back through the beads and tighten the wire. Check the fit, and add or remove beads if necessary. Crimp the crimp bead.

5 Wrap the second strand around the first. Add or remove beads from the second strand if necessary.

6 Remove the tape from the second strand and string a crimp bead, an 8°, and the jump ring. Go back through the beads and tighten the wire. Crimp the crimp bead and trim the excess wire.

2 String a top-drilled rectangle, a 6°, a pearl, a 6°, a cylinder bead, a 6°, a pearl, and a 6°. Repeat the pattern until the bracelet is the desired length. Tape the end.

materials

two-strand bracelet 7 in. (18cm)
- 5–7 10 x 8mm faceted top-drilled rectangle carnelian beads
- 10–15 5–6mm potato-shaped pearls, peach
- 30–40 size 6° seed beads, matte black
- 24–28 size 8° seed beads, amber
- 2g Japanese cylinder beads, mint green
- lobster claw clasp
- flexible beading wire, .014 or .015
- 4 crimp beads
- 6mm soldered jump ring
- chainnose pliers
- diagonal wire cutters
- crimping pliers (optional)

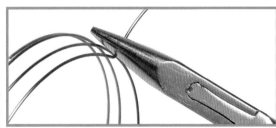

1 **memory wire bracelet** • Separate four coils of memory wire from the stack of coils. Instead of cutting the wire, hold it with chainnose pliers and bend it back and forth at one place until the wire breaks. Don't use jewelry-weight wire cutters on memory wire; the wire will ruin the blades.

3 String eight petal-shaped beads, a pearl, an 8° seed bead, a faceted round, an 8°, and a pearl. Repeat the pattern until you are 2 in. (5cm) from the end of the memory wire.

3 Attach the remaining wire to the clasp as in step 1. String six cylinder beads, an 8°, a 6°, and an 8° on the wire. Repeat the pattern until the bracelet is the desired length. Tape the end.

memory wire bracelet 4 coils
- 10 x 8mm faceted rectangle carnelian pendant
- 2 8-in. (20cm) strands petal-shaped beads, black
- 20–24 5–6mm potato-shaped pearls, peach
- 10–12 6mm faceted round beads, orange
- 1g size 8° seed beads, melon
- memory wire, bracelet diameter
- chainnose pliers
- roundnose pliers
- heavy-duty wire cutters (optional)

2 Using roundnose pliers, make a small loop on one end of the memory wire.

4 To finish the bracelet, string eight petal-shaped beads, a pearl, the pendant, a pearl, and a petal-shaped bead. Make sure there are no spaces between beads. Make a small loop at the end of the wire.

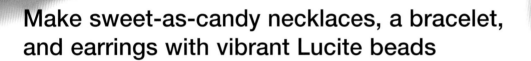

Make sweet-as-candy necklaces, a bracelet, and earrings with vibrant Lucite beads

Orange
Yellow

by Naomi Fujimoto

inspiration fabric

The colors of this retro fabric are as fun and playful as its cartoonlike graphics; content and color are well matched. The jewelry follows suit: brightly colored Lucite beads create casual pieces perfect for spring and summer soirees. In each piece, the predominantly red-orange-yellow spectrum has a complementary color thrown in: purple to complement yellow, and green for red. Whenever you want to add a splash of contrast to a palette with a dominant color scheme, choose its complement.

One pre-packaged assortment of Lucite contained enough beads in a variety of styles and colors to make the necklaces, bracelet, and earrings shown here.

materials

hoop-pendant necklace 16½ in. (41.9cm)
- Lucite beads (The Beadin' Path, 877-922-3237, beadinpath.com)
  27mm hoop beads
  6–10 16mm round beads
  6–10 14mm round beads
  8–12 10mm round beads, in 2 colors or finishes
- **22–34** 6mm round crystals, in 2 colors
- size 11º seed bead
- lobster claw clasp with soldered jump ring
- flexible beading wire, .014 or .015
- 4 3mm round spacers
- 9–10mm (inside diameter) 16-gauge jump ring
- 2 crimp beads
- chainnose pliers
- roundnose pliers
- crimping pliers (optional)
- diagonal wire cutters

cherry-and-citrus necklace 15½ in. (39.4cm)
- Lucite beads (The Beadin' Path)
  7–9 19 x 23mm cherry beads
  4–6 14mm round beads
  4–6 12 x 16mm oval beads
  14–20 10mm round beads, in 2 colors or finishes
- **14–18** 6mm round crystals, in 2 colors
- lobster claw clasp with soldered jump ring
- flexible beading wire, .014 or .015
- 4 3mm round spacers
- 2 crimp beads
- chainnose or crimping pliers
- diagonal wire cutters

bracelet 7 in. (18cm)
- Lucite beads (The Beadin' Path)
  5–8 16mm round beads
  10–15 14mm round beads, in 2 colors
  3–6 12 x 16mm oval beads
  5–10 10mm round beads, in 2 colors
  5–10 8 x 14mm fruit beads
- **6–8** 8mm round crystals
- **6–8** 6mm round crystals
- lobster claw clasp with 4–5mm jump ring
- **8–10** in. (20–25cm) cable chain, 4mm links
- **35–55** 1½-in. (3.8cm) 20-gauge head pins
- **5–10** 4mm 18-gauge jump rings
- chainnose pliers
- roundnose pliers
- diagonal wire cutters

earrings
- Lucite beads (The Beadin' Path)
  2 27mm hoop beads
  2 10mm round beads
- 2 6mm round crystals
- 4 1½-in. head pins or 6 in. (15cm) 22-gauge sterling silver wire, half-hard
- 2 9–10mm (inside diameter) 16-gauge jump rings
- pair of earring wires
- chainnose pliers
- roundnose pliers
- diagonal wire cutters

1 hoop-pendant necklace • Determine the finished length of your necklace (this one is 16½ in./41.9cm), add 6 in. (15cm), and cut a piece of beading wire to that length. Open a 9–10mm jump ring (see Basics, p. 8). String the hoop bead and close the jump ring. Center the pendant and an 11º seed bead on the wire.

2 On each end of the beading wire, string a pattern of Lucite beads alternating with crystals. Repeat until the necklace is 1 in. (2.5cm) short of the desired length.

3 On one end, string a 3mm round spacer, a crimp bead, a spacer, and the clasp. Go back through the beads just strung plus one more and tighten the wire. Repeat at the other end, substituting a jump ring for the clasp. Check the fit, and add or remove an equal number of beads from each end if necessary. Crimp the crimp beads (Basics) and trim the excess wire.

editor's tip

Like all vintage beads, Lucite beads may not always be available in every size, shape, and color. Make sure you have enough beads to finish your projects before you start.

1 cherry-and-citrus necklace •
Determine the finished length of your necklace (this one is 15½ in./39.4cm), add 6 in. (15cm), and cut a piece of beading wire to that length. Center a cherry bead between two crystals on the wire.

2 On each end, string a 10mm matte bead, a 14mm, a 10mm glossy, a crystal, a cherry, and a crystal. (Use crystals in a different color from those in step 1.)

3 On each end, string a 10mm matte, an oval, a 10mm glossy, a crystal, a cherry, and a crystal. (String the same color crystals as in step 1.)

Repeat steps 2 and 3 on each end until the necklace is 1 in. (2.5cm) short of the desired length. Finish as in step 3 of the hoop-pendant necklace.

1 **bracelet** • String each Lucite bead and crystal on a head pin. Make a plain loop (Basics) above each bead. String each fruit bead on a jump ring. Make a total of 40–65 dangles. (The size of the chain links and the bracelet length determine how many dangles you need.)

2 Determine the finished length of your bracelet (this one is 7 in./18cm), add 1½ in. (3.8cm), and cut a piece of chain to that length.

3 Open a dangle's jump ring or loop, attach it to a link, and close the jump ring. Attach one dangle per link until the bracelet is the desired length. You should have about 1½ in. of chain without dangles.

4 Use a jump ring to attach the clasp to the end link at the end with dangles. Check the fit, and add or remove dangles if necessary. Trim the chain at the other end so you have 1 in. (2.5cm) without beads for an extender. Attach one or two dangles to the end link.

1 **earrings** • Open a 9–10mm jump ring. Attach a hoop bead and close the jump ring.

2 Trim the heads from two 1½-in. (3.8cm) head pins or cut two pieces of 22-gauge wire to that length. On one wire, string a 10mm bead and make a plain loop at each end.

3 On the other wire, string a crystal and make a plain loop at each end. Make these loops perpendicular to each other.

4 Open each loop on the 10mm-bead unit. Attach one loop to the jump ring and the other to a crystal unit's loop. Close the loops.

5 Open an earring wire. String the crystal unit's top loop and close the earring wire. Make a second earring to match the first.

Orange
Yellow

Link delicate crystal charms with jump rings for a flowery cuff and earrings

by Jane Konkel

materials

bracelet 7 in. (18cm)
- crystal flower charms
  (Rings & Things,
  rings-things.com.)
  21 9mm, hyacinth
  21 9mm, jonquil
  14 9mm, topaz
- four-strand slide clasp
- **106** 4mm oval jump rings
- 2 pairs chainnose pliers

earrings
- crystal flower charms
  8 9mm, hyacinth
  8 9mm, jonquil
  4 9mm, topaz
- **20** 4mm oval jump rings
- pair of earring wires
- 2 pairs of chainnose pliers

inspiration
decorative art

You never know where inspiration lurks. . . you might find it in something as mundane as a set of retro drink coasters. This sixties-era floral motif pairs ambers and deep oranges in a surprisingly fresh combination. The colors are side by side on the color wheel, which makes for a harmonious and pleasing design.

Columns of linked charms form a lighthearted bracelet and earrings ensemble.

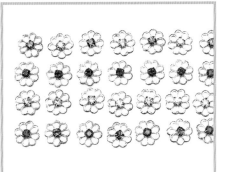

1 bracelet • Arrange crystal flower charms so you have 14 across by four deep (for a 7-in./18cm bracelet). Increase or decrease the number of columns to adjust the length.

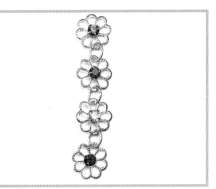

2 Open three jump rings (see Basics, p. 8) and connect a column of four flowers. Close the jump rings. Repeat with the remaining columns.

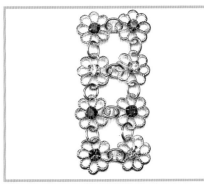

3 Use jump rings to connect the flowers in one column to the flowers beside them in the next column.

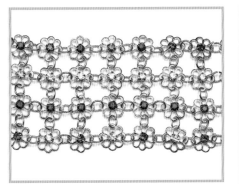

4 Repeat step 3 until you have connected all the flowers.

5 Attach each of the two middle flowers to their respective loops on the slide clasp with one jump ring each. Attach the outer flowers to the outer loops with two jump rings each. Repeat at the other end. (Be sure the second half of the clasp is correctly oriented before you attach it.)

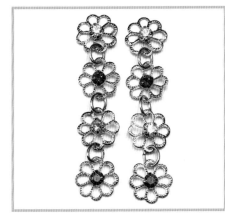

1 earrings • Open three jump rings and connect four crystal flower charms. Close the jump rings. Repeat.

2 Attach a jump ring to the top of each flower at the top of the columns. Connect these two jump rings to an unattached flower, as shown. Repeat with the flowers at the bottom of the columns.

3 Open the loop on an earring wire and attach it to the top flower's center loop. Close the earring wire's loop. Make a second earring to match the first.

seven-drop dangle

double dangle

eight-drop dangle

long dangle

Yellow

Tiny drop beads build a wardrobe of playful earrings

Taking its lead from the range of attention-grabbing yellows found in a bouquet of summer daisies – ambers to orange-yellows to pure yellow – this color scheme grew into a compelling analogous palette. To translate the cheerful energy of daisies into your jewelry, suspend drops in sunshine colors from a variety of gold earring findings.

by Diane Jolie

inspiration nature

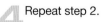

1 seven-drop dangle • Thread a needle on each end of a 14-in. (36cm) piece of C-Lon. Center one yellow drop bead on the thread. On both needles, pick up a brown and a green 11º seed bead.

2 On one needle, pick up a matte yellow drop and a green 11º. On the other needle, pick up a brown 11º and a matte yellow drop.

3 Using both needles together, pick up a brown 11º, a yellow drop, and a green 11º.

4 Repeat step 2.

5 Repeat step 3, then pick up a brown 11º and a green 11º.

6 Pick up a soldered jump ring on one needle. Tie the threads together with a surgeon's knot (see Basics, p. 8). Glue the knot. Take both threads through several 11ºs and trim the tails. Connect the jump ring to an earring wire. Make a second earring to match the first.

Long and short earrings drenched in yellows and oranges dangle from gold earring wires. Note the subtle greens and browns in the daisies that also show up in the seed beads.

1 eight-drop dangle • Make a seven-drop dangle as described at left, substituting orange-yellow drops for the yellow drops. Omit the last three 11ºs; instead, pick up a matte yellow drop. Make a second earring to match the first.

1 long dangle • Repeat steps 1–5 of the seven-drop dangle, substituting orange-yellow drops for the first and third yellow drops. Omit the last two 11º seed beads in step 5.

2 Repeat step 2 of the seven-drop dangle. On both needles, pick up a brown 11º, a yellow drop, an orange-yellow drop, a yellow drop, a green 11º, a brown 11º, and a green 11º. Attach a soldered jump ring and secure the thread, as in step 6.

3 Open a 3mm jump ring (Basics). Attach the dangle's soldered jump ring to the drop finding's lower loop. Close the jump ring. Slide the finding's top loop onto an earring wire. Make a second earring to match the first.

materials

all projects
- C-Lon beading thread
- beading needles, size #12
- G-S Hypo Cement or clear nail polish

seven-drop dangle
- 6 6mm drop beads, yellow
- 8 6mm drop beads, matte yellow
- size 11º seed beads
  12 brown
  12 green
- pair of decorative earring wires (Rishashay, 800-517-3311, rishashay.com)
- 2 3mm soldered jump rings

eight-drop dangle
- 6 6mm drop beads, orange-yellow
- 10 6mm drop beads, matte yellow
- size 11º seed beads
  8 brown
  10 green
- pair of decorative earring wires (Rishashay)
- 2 3mm soldered jump rings

long dangle
- 6 6mm drop beads, orange-yellow
- 6 6mm drop beads, yellow
- 12 6mm drop beads, matte yellow
- size 11º seed beads
  16 brown
  16 green
- pair of earring wires
- 2 26mm round drop findings (Fire Mountain Gems, 800-355-2137, firemountaingems.com)
- 2 3mm soldered jump rings
- 2 3mm jump rings
- 2 pairs of chainnose pliers, or chainnose and bentnose pliers

double dangle
- 8 6mm drop beads, yellow
- 16 6mm drop beads, matte yellow
- size 11º seed beads
  22 brown
  22 green
- pair of earring wires
- 2 3mm soldered jump rings

1 double dangle • Repeat steps 1–5 of the seven-drop dangle.

2 Center a new 14-in. (36cm) piece of C-Lon in the bottom drop, as shown, and pick up a brown and a green 11º on both needles, as in step 1 of the seven-drop dangle.

3 Repeat step 2 of the seven-drop dangle. On both needles, pick up a brown 11º, go through the next yellow drop on the first dangle, and pick up a green 11º.

4 Repeat step 3, omitting the last 11º. Finish the dangle as in step 6 of the seven-drop dangle.

Yellow

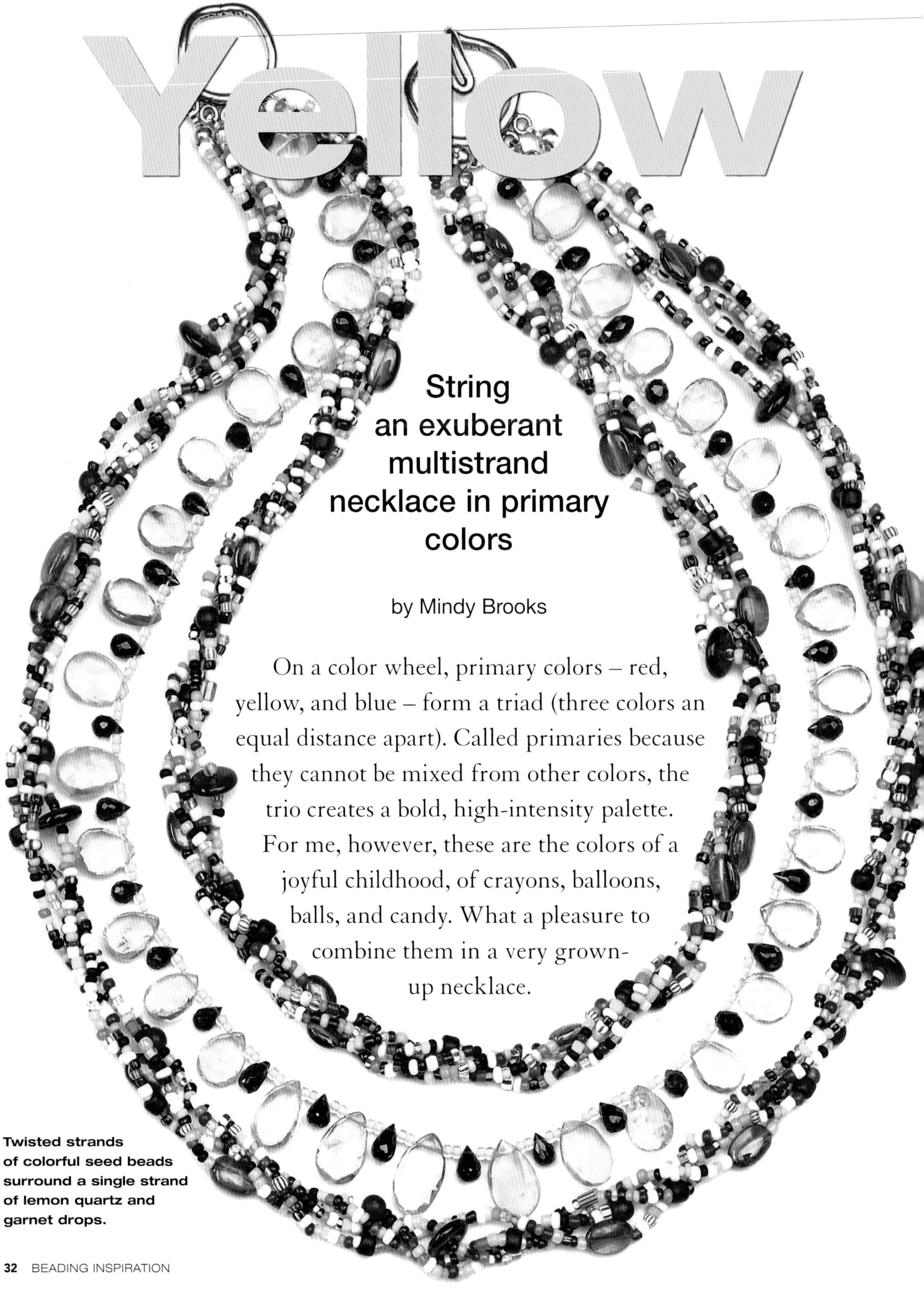

String
an exuberant
multistrand
necklace in primary
colors

by Mindy Brooks

On a color wheel, primary colors – red, yellow, and blue – form a triad (three colors an equal distance apart). Called primaries because they cannot be mixed from other colors, the trio creates a bold, high-intensity palette. For me, however, these are the colors of a joyful childhood, of crayons, balloons, balls, and candy. What a pleasure to combine them in a very grown-up necklace.

Twisted strands of colorful seed beads surround a single strand of lemon quartz and garnet drops.

1 Determine the finished length of the inner group of seed bead strands. (These are 16½ in./41.9cm before twisting.) Double this number, add 8 in. (20cm), and cut two pieces of nylon cord to this length.

2 Center a seed bead on one strand. Tie a square knot (see Basics, p. 8) around the bead. Hold the two cut ends together and string a bead tip with the hook end toward the seed bead. Pull on the cords until the seed bead sits inside the bead tip.

3 Close the bead tip with chainnose pliers.

4 Thread a needle on one cord and string a random mix of seed beads, adding accent beads as desired. When the strand is the desired length, tape the end to secure the beads. Repeat with the other cord. Add or remove beads as necessary until the strands are the same length.

5 Remove the tape and string a bead tip, hook end pointing away from the beads, over both cut ends. String a seed bead on one cord and slide it into the bead tip. Tie the threads together with several square knots around the bead, glue the knots, and close the bead tip. Trim the excess cord.

6 Repeat steps 2–5 to prepare a second set of beaded strands the same length as the first set.

7 Using roundnose pliers, gently bend one bead tip's hook into a circle. Attach it to the clasp's top loop and close the hook. Repeat with the bead tip on the second set of beaded strands, working in the clasp's next loop.

8 Hold the ends of the strands in each hand. Twist the strands together six or seven times, or as required to reach your desired length. (These twisted strands are 16 in./41cm.) Attach the bead tips to the remaining clasp half, as in step 7. Make sure the clasp halves line up correctly before you attach the bead tips.

materials

multistrand necklace 16 in. (41cm)

- 16-in. (41cm) strand lemon quartz, teardrops or briolettes
- 16-in. strand garnet briolettes
- assorted 4–8mm glass accent beads
- 40g seed beads in yellow, red, blue, black, and white or 2 30g tubes mixed Czech seed beads (Knot Just Beads, 414-771-8360)
- 5g size 11º seed beads, light yellow

- five-strand clasp
- nylon cord, 1/0x
- flexible beading wire, .010–.012
- beading needles, #10
- 10 bead tips
- 2 crimp beads
- G-S Hypo Cement
- chainnose pliers
- roundnose pliers
- crimping pliers

inspiration color wheel

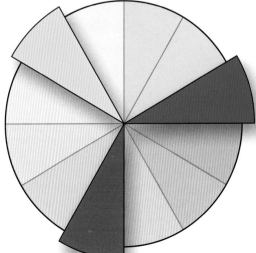

9 Cut a piece of beading wire 6 in. (15cm) longer than your beaded strands. String a crimp bead and a bead tip, hook end toward the crimp bead, on the end of the beading wire. Crimp the crimp bead (Basics) and test it to make sure it holds. Trim the wire close to the crimp bead. Slide the crimp bead into the bead tip and close the bead tip as before.

10 String an alternating pattern of teardrops and briolettes separated by pairs of yellow 11º seed beads. For the gemstone strand to fall slightly below the seed bead strands, string it about ½ in. (1.3cm) longer. (This one is 16½ in.)

11 When you reach the desired length, string a bead tip, hook end pointing away from the gemstones, and a crimp bead. Slide the crimp bead into the bead tip and close up any spaces between beads. Crimp the crimp bead securely, trim the excess wire, and close the bead tip. Attach the bead tips to the center clasp loops, as in step 7.

12 For the last set of beaded strands, repeat steps 1–8, using cords that are long enough to drape about ½ in. below the gemstone strand when twisted. (These are 19 in./48cm before twisting.) Attach the bead tips to the remaining clasp loops.

Yellow Green

Link round and square mother-of-pearl beads in a necklace with a custom clasp

by Linda Augsburg

At first glance, the muted tones of autumn pears on a bolt of cotton seemed an unlikely candidate to inspire a piece of jewelry. Yet, the striated yellow-greens on mother-of-pearl squares looked remarkably similar to the pears' shading. For accents, leaf beads and mosaic beads reflect the soft browns of the pears' stems and shadows. The result is a necklace in warm, low-intensity colors, an ideal palette for tailored fall clothing.

inspiration
fabric

Bronze-colored wire supports an alternating pattern of square green and faceted golden-brown beads. Glass leaves dangle from an unusual double loop.

materials

necklace 17½ in. (44.5cm)
- **12** 16 x 16mm flat rectangular dyed mother-of-pearl beads
- **22** 9 x 9mm pressed-glass leaf beads
- **11** 6mm round mosaic mother-of-pearl beads
- bronze-colored copper craft wire
  7 ft. (2.1m) 22-gauge
  1 ft. (30cm) 20-gauge
- chainnose pliers
- roundnose pliers
- bentnose pliers (optional)
- nylon jaw pliers (optional)
- diagonal wire cutters

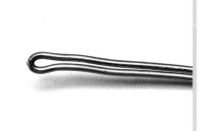

1 **clasp** • To make the clasp's hook, cut a 6-in. (15cm) piece of 20-gauge wire. Fold the wire in half, making the fold as tight as possible. Smooth the wire by pulling it through nylon jaw pliers (optional).

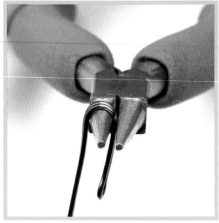

2 Use roundnose pliers to make a bend in the wires about ⅝ in. (1.6cm) from the fold.

3 Make a wrapped loop (see Basics, p. 8) using both cut ends of the wires as if they were one. Trim the wires close to the wraps.

4 To make the clasp's eye, cut a 6-in. piece of 20-gauge wire. Grasp the center of the wire with roundnose pliers, and cross the wires around one jaw to make a loop. Reposition the loop as shown, and wrap the wires around the jaw to form a second loop. Cross the wire tails below the jaw.

5 Hold both loops in chainnose pliers, and twist the tails once so the tails are perpendicular to the loops.

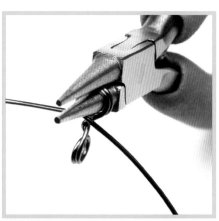

6 Wrap each wire tail around one jaw of the roundnose pliers to form a second pair of loops. Be sure to leave a small space between the two loops.

7 Hold the second pair of loops with chainnose or bentnose pliers, and wrap the tails around the wires between the two loops. Trim the excess wire.

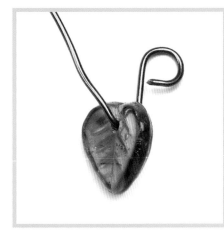

1 **necklace •** Cut a 2-in. (5cm) piece of 22-gauge wire. Make a loop at one end. String a leaf bead on the wire and bend the wire tail up around the bead.

2 Put the first loop back on your roundnose pliers. Bring the wire tail around the jaw in the opposite direction of the first loop, forming a figure 8. Trim the wire under the second loop.

3 Press the two loops together with chainnose pliers so they look like one two-wire loop. Make a total of 22 leaf dangles.

4 Cut a 1½-in. (3.8cm) piece of 22-gauge wire. Make a plain loop (Basics) at one end. String a 6mm bead on the wire and make a plain loop at the other end. Make a total of 12 6mm bead units and 12 16mm bead units.

5 Open the loops on the 6mm units. Attach a leaf unit and a 16mm unit to each loop, forming a linked chain of alternating 6mm units and 16mm units. Close the loops. Note: Depending on the orientation of the 6mm unit's loop, you may need to attach either the leaf unit or the 16mm bead unit first. Add units until the necklace is 1½ in. short of the desired length.

6 Open the loop on the end units and attach a clasp half to each unit.

Yellow Green

Playful shapes and bright colors combine for fun and flirty jewelry

by Helene Tsigistras

The yellow-green of changing leaves suggests early autumn skies and crisp, cool temperatures. The luminescent shell beads in this necklace, bracelet, and earrings set capture the bright colors and energy of the upcoming season.

inspiration nature

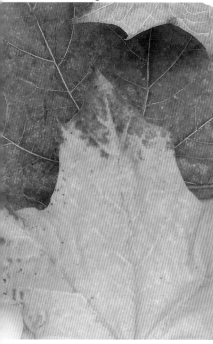

Subtle brown wood beads are a good foil for the vivid colors of leaves.

1 necklace • String a yellow star and a 6mm round bead on a head pin. Make a wrapped loop (see Basics, p. 8) above the beads. Make four more star units.

2 Determine the finished length of your necklace (this one is 20 in./51cm), add six in. (15cm), and cut a piece of flexible beading wire to that length. Center a star unit on the wire.

3 String a 6mm, an oval, a 6mm, an oval, and a 6mm on one end of the wire. Repeat on the other side of the star unit.

5 Repeat steps 3 and 4. On each end string a 6mm, an oval, a 6mm, an oval, a 6mm, an oval, a 6mm, and a star.

materials

all projects
- chainnose pliers
- roundnose pliers
- diagonal wire cutters

necklace 20 in. (51cm)
- **7** 14mm star-shaped shell beads, yellow
- **20** 10 x 13mm oval shell beads, yellow-green
- **33** 6mm round beads, brown
- toggle clasp
- flexible beading wire, .012–.015
- **2** crimp beads
- **2** 2-in. 24-gauge head pins
- crimping pliers

bracelet 8¼ in. (21cm)
- **12** 14mm star-shaped shell beads, yellow
- **9** 10 x 13mm oval shell beads, yellow-green
- **16** 6mm round beads, brown

- toggle clasp
- flexible beading wire, .012–.015
- **2** crimp beads
- **2** crimp covers (optional)
- crimping pliers

long dangle earrings
- **2** 14mm star-shaped shell beads, yellow
- **2** 6mm round beads, brown
- **2** in. cable chain, 2mm
- **2** 2-in. head pins
- pair earring wires

circle earrings
- **2** 14mm star-shaped shell beads, yellow
- **2** 40mm shell ring findings, yellow-green
- **2** 6mm round beads, brown
- **4** in. 24-gauge sterling silver wire
- **2** 2-in. head pins
- pair earring wires

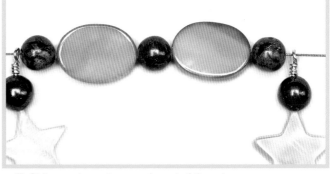

4 String a star unit on each end of the wire.

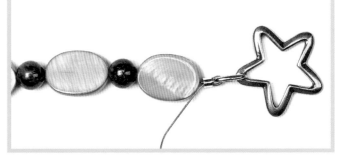

6 String an alternating pattern of 6mm and ovals on each end until your necklace is within 1 in. (2.5cm) of the desired length. String a crimp bead and the loop of a clasp half on each end. Go back through the crimp bead, tighten the wires, crimp the crimp beads (Basics), and trim the tails.

1 **bracelet •** Determine the finished length of your bracelet (this one is 8¼ in./21cm), add 5 in. (13cm), and cut two pieces of flexible beading wire to that length. String a crimp bead and the loop of a clasp half over both strands. Go back through the crimp bead, tighten the wire, and crimp.

2 Separate the wires. On one wire, string a 6mm, two stars, a 6mm, and an oval. Repeat this pattern until the bracelet is within 1 in. of the desired length.

3 On the second wire, string a 6mm, a star, a 6mm, and two ovals. Repeat the pattern until the strand is within 1 in. of the desired length.

4 String a crimp bead and the loop of the other clasp half over both wires. Go back through the crimp bead, tighten the wires, and crimp. Trim the tails.

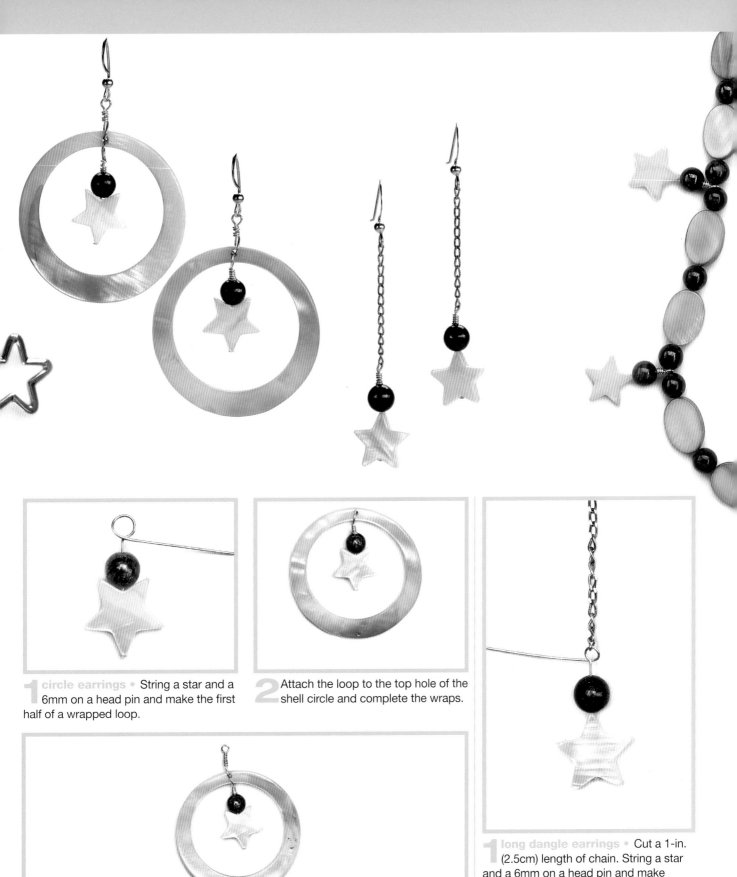

1 circle earrings • String a star and a 6mm on a head pin and make the first half of a wrapped loop.

2 Attach the loop to the top hole of the shell circle and complete the wraps.

3 Cut a 2-in. length of wire and make the first half of a wrapped loop. Attach the loop to the top hole of the circle unit and complete the wraps. Make a wrapped loop on the other end of the wire, wrapping until the coils meet. Open the loop on an earring wire and attach the unit. Close the loop. Make a second earring to match the first.

1 long dangle earrings • Cut a 1-in. (2.5cm) length of chain. String a star and a 6mm on a head pin and make the first half of a wrapped loop. Attach the loop to the chain and complete the wraps. Open the loop (Basics) on an earring finding and attach the other end of the chain. Close the loop. Make a second earring to match the first.

A long-time favorite of jewelry designers, tourmaline gems come in a dramatic sweep from near-black to green to pink. Look for deep, rich colors when you purchase a strand.

Colors opposite each other on the color wheel are called complements, and they spring to life when used together. This is also true with the color relationship known as split complements, a trio consisting of one color plus the colors on each side of its complement. Lucky for us, these colors occur naturally in tourmalines. Rich greens flourish next to luscious raspberry and orange tones in a range of values and intensity.

inspiration
color wheel

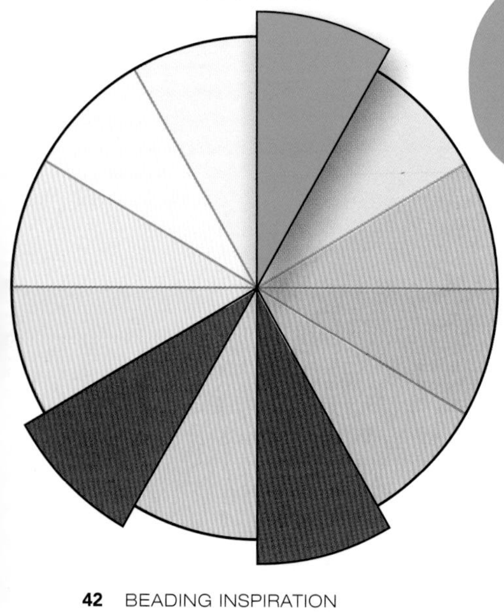

Green

Create a necklace, bracelet, and earrings ensemble with tourmaline nuggets and chips

by Naomi Fujimoto

1 necklace • String a pink tourmaline nugget on a decorative head pin. Make a wrapped loop (see Basics, p. 8) above the bead.

2 Determine the finished length of your necklace, (this one is 16 in./41cm.), add 6 in. (15cm), and cut two pieces of beading wire to that length. On one wire, string chips interspersed with 11º seed beads until the strand is 1 in. (2.5cm) short of the desired length. End with a chip.

editor's tip

Before making the necklace, set aside five pairs of matching chips for the earrings.

3 On the other wire, center the pendant and an 11º. On each end, string chips interspersed with 11ºs until the strand is 1 in. short of the desired length. End with a chip.

4 On each end of each strand, string a round spacer, a crimp bead, a round spacer, and half the clasp. Go back through the beads just strung and tighten the wires. Check the fit, and add or remove beads if necessary. Crimp the crimp beads (Basics) and trim the excess wire.

materials

necklace 16 in. (41cm)
- 12–15mm pink tourmaline nugget
- 2 16-in. (41cm) strands 4–7mm tourmaline chips
- 8 3mm round spacers
- 2g size 11º seed beads
- toggle clasp
- flexible beading wire, .014 or .015
- 4 crimp beads
- 2-in. (5cm) decorative head pin
- chainnose pliers
- roundnose pliers
- crimping pliers (optional)
- diagonal wire cutters

bracelet 7 in. (18cm)
- 15-in. (38cm) strand 12–15mm tourmaline nuggets
- 12–16 4mm flat spacers
- ribbon elastic
- twisted-wire needles
- G-S Hypo Cement

earrings
- 10 4–7mm tourmaline chips
- 8 4mm flat spacers
- pair of 1-in. (2.5cm) beading hoops
- chainnose pliers
- diagonal wire cutters

1 bracelet • Determine the finished length of your bracelet, add 3 in. (7.6cm), and double that measurement. Cut a piece of ribbon elastic to that length. Center a needle on the elastic and tape the ends together. String an alternating pattern of nuggets and spacers until the bracelet is the desired length.

2 Tie the ends with a surgeon's knot (Basics). Glue the knot and trim the ends to ⅛ in. (3mm). Gently stretch the bracelet to pull the knot into an adjacent spacer.

1 earrings • String an alternating pattern of five chips and four spacers on a beading hoop. With chainnose pliers, bend the wire up ¼ in. (6mm) from the hoop's end. Make a second earring to match the first.

Green

Soothing colors combine for a lovely necklace, bracelet, and earrings set

by Helene Tsigistras

The translucent materials and geometric patterns of a shell and wire candle-holder are re-created in soft shades of aventurine, amethyst, and shimmering shell. The defined shapes and cool tones of the gemstones contrast with the organic shapes and warm tones of the shell beads – a distinct, yet harmonious, combination.

inspiration
decorative art

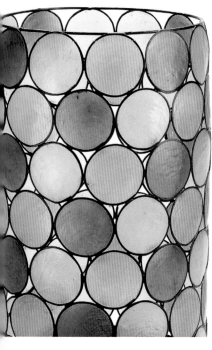

Translucent colors and soft shades keep this multistrand necklace light and airy.

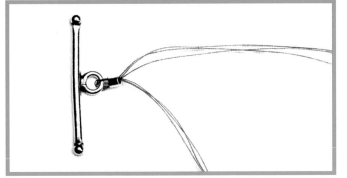

1 necklace • Determine the finished length of your necklace (this one is 23½ in./59.7cm), add 6 in. (15cm), and cut three strands of flexible beading wire to that length. String a crimp bead and half the clasp over all three wires, and go back through the crimp bead. Tighten the wires and crimp the crimp bead (see Basics, p. 8).

2 String a 4mm black bead and a 7mm amethyst circle over all three wires.

materials

all projects
• chainnose pliers
• roundnose pliers
• diagonal wire cutters

necklace 23½ in. (60cm)
• 4 15 x 17mm diamond shells, gold
• 3 16-in. strands 3 x 8mm rectangles, aventurine
• 16-in. strand 8mm circles, amethyst
• 10 4mm round beads, black
• toggle clasp
• flexible beading wire, .014–.015
• 2 crimp beads
• crimping pliers

Y-necklace 24½ in. (62.2cm)
• 15 x 17mm diamond shell, gold
• 11 3 x 8mm rectangles, aventurine
• 8mm circle, amethyst
• 22 in. (56cm) large-link chain
• 7 in. (18cm) 24-gauge wire
• 8 2-in. head pins
• lobster claw clasp

bracelet 7½ in. (19cm)
• 3 15 x 17mm diamond shells, gold
• 22 3 x 8mm rectangles, aventurine
• 2 8mm circles, amethyst
• 8 4mm round beads, black
• toggle clasp
• flexible beading wire, .014–.015
• 2 crimp beads
• crimping pliers

earrings
• 2 15 x 17mm diamond shells, gold
• 6 3 x 8mm rectangles, aventurine
• 2 8mm circles, amethyst
• 2 in. cable chain, 3mm
• 24 in. 24-gauge wire
• 8 2-in. head pins
• pair earring wires

3 Separate the wires and string a random pattern of 3 x 8mm aventurine rectangles and amethyst circles for 4 in. (10cm) on each strand, beginning and ending with a rectangle.

4 String a 4mm, a shell, and a 4mm over all three wires.

5 Separate the wires and string an assortment of rectangles and circles on each strand for 3 in. (7.6cm).

6 Repeat steps 4 and 5 twice. Then string a 4mm, a shell, and a 4mm over all three wires. Repeat step 3. String a circle, a 4mm, and a crimp bead over all three wires. Go through the other clasp half and back through the crimp bead. Tighten the wires, crimp the crimp bead, and trim the tails.

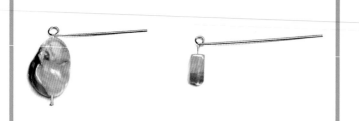

1 **Y-necklace** • String a shell bead on a head pin and make the first half of a wrapped loop (Basics). String a rectangle on another head pin and make the first half of a wrapped loop. Make six more rectangle units.

2 Cut a 1-in. length of chain. Attach the shell unit to the bottom link of chain and finish the wraps. Attach the rectangle units to each link of the chain, spacing them evenly along the sides. Finish the wraps.

3 Cut a 2-in. (6.4cm) piece of wire. Make the first half of a wrapped loop and attach it to the top link of the chain dangle. Finish the wraps. String a circle and make the first half of a wrapped loop above the bead.

4 Cut a 4¼-in. (10.8cm) length of chain. Find the center link, and attach the dangle. Complete the wraps.

5 Cut a 2¼-in. (5.7cm) piece of chain. Cut a 2-in. piece of wire and make the first half of a wrapped loop. Attach it to one end of the chain unit from step 3 and complete the wraps. String a rectangle on the wire and make the first half of a wrapped loop. Attach the end link of chain segment and complete the wraps. Repeat on the other side of the necklace.

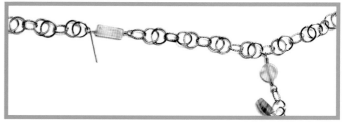

6 Cut a 6-in. (15cm) piece of chain. Cut a 2-in. piece of wire and make the first half of a wrapped loop. Attach it to one end of the necklace and complete the wraps. String a rectangle bead on the wire and make the first half of a wrapped loop. Attach the end link of a 6-in. chain segment and complete the wraps. Repeat on the other side of the necklace.

7 Open a jump ring (Basics), and attach a lobster claw clasp to one end of the necklace. Close the jump ring. Repeat on the other end of the necklace with a soldered jump ring.

1 **bracelet** • Determine the finished length of your bracelet (this one is 7½ in./19.1cm), add 5 in. (13cm), and cut three pieces of flexible beading wire to that length. String a crimp bead and the loop of one clasp half over all three strands. Go back through the crimp bead, tighten the wires, and crimp.

2 String a 4mm over all three wires. Separate the wires and string a rectangle on each wire. String a 4mm over all three wires.

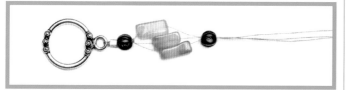

3 String a shell and a 4mm over all three wires.

4 Separate the wires. String three rectangles on a wire. Repeat with a second wire. On the third wire, string a rectangle, a circle, and a rectangle. String a 4mm over all three wires.

5 Repeat steps 3 and 4 twice. Then string a shell and a 4mm. Separate the wires and string a rectangle on each. String a 4mm, a crimp bead, and the loop of the other clasp half over all three wires. Go back through the crimp bead, tighten the wires, crimp the crimp bead, and trim the tails.

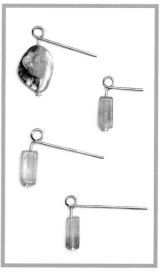

1 **earrings** • String a small shell bead on a head pin and make the first half of a wrapped loop. String a rectangle on another head pin and make the first half of a wrapped loop. Make two more rectangle units.

2 Cut a 1-in. length of chain. Attach the shell unit to the bottom link and complete the wraps. At the other end of the chain, skip the top link and attach a rectangle unit to each of the next three links, alternating sides, and complete the wraps.

3 Cut a 2-in. (5cm) piece of 24-gauge wire and make a wrapped loop. String a circle and make the first half of a wrapped loop. Attach the unit to the top link of the chain unit, and complete the wraps. Open the loop on an earring wire and attach the earring. Make a second earring to match the first.

Green Blue

String a two-strand gemstone necklace with a dangling centerpiece

by Paulette Biedenbender

Designers look for classic color schemes they can use again and again. This cool-color twosome taken from a fabric swatch is sure to be a contender. The cool blue essence of water pairs gracefully with the vibrance of spring's freshest greens. Not only are greens and blues neighbors on the color wheel, these two also are similar in color value – attributes that lend harmony to the finished piece.

*inspiration*fabric

Use chain to create a dynamic centerpiece of gems, crystals, and shell beads.

1 On each of four head pins, string a crystal, a flat spacer, a tube-shaped opal, a flat spacer, and a crystal. Make a plain loop (see Basics, p. 8). On each of four head pins, string a crystal, a bead cap, an 8mm round, a bead cap, and a crystal. Make a plain loop as before. On each of five head pins, string three 4mm rounds. Make a plain loop as before.

2 Cut a 1¾-in. (4.4cm) length of chain. Open the loop (Basics) on an 8mm round dangle and a tube dangle. Attach both to the same end link. Close the loops. Attach the remaining dangles to the chain links as shown.

3 Cut two 3½-in. (8.9cm) lengths of 22-gauge wire. On each wire, make a wrapped loop (Basics) on one end. On each wire, string a crystal, a bead cap, an 8mm round, a bead cap, and a crystal. Make the first half of a wrapped loop above the crystals.

4 Attach the unfinished loops on both bead units to the top chain link. Complete the wraps.

materials

necklace 16¾ in. (42.5cm)

- 16-in. (41cm) strands of the following:
  5 x 7mm (approximately) flat ovals, blue Peruvian opal
  5 x 8mm (approximately) tubes, blue Peruvian opal
  4mm rounds, green dyed shell
- 8 8mm faceted rounds, green dyed jade
- 44 4mm round crystals, chrysolite AB
- 16 7mm bead caps
- 8 7mm flat spacers
- 4 4 x 2mm spacers, large-hole
- 8 3 x 2mm spacers, large-hole
- two-strand toggle clasp
- 2 in. (5cm) twisted-cable chain, 5.5mm
- 7 in. (18cm) 22-gauge wire, half-hard
- 13 2-in. (5cm) head pins
- flexible beading wire, .014 or .015
- 6 crimp beads
- chainnose pliers
- roundnose pliers
- crimping pliers
- diagonal wire cutters

5 Determine the finished length of your necklace. (This one is 16¾ in./ 42.5cm). Divide that measurement in half, add 6 in. (15cm), and cut four pieces of beading wire to that length.

6 String a crimp bead and the loop of a bead unit over two pieces of beading wire. Go back through the crimp bead and tighten the wire. Make a folded crimp (Basics).

7 String two 4 x 2mm spacers over both tails and wires and slide the spacers over the folded crimp. Then string a bead cap, an 8mm round, and a bead cap. Separate the wires and string a crystal on each.

8 Repeat steps 6 and 7 at the other end of the necklace with the other two wires.

9 On one wire on each end, string a flat opal, a 4mm round, a tube-shaped opal, a 4mm round, a flat opal, a crystal, a tube-shaped opal, and a 4mm round. On the other wire on each end, string a tube-shaped opal, a 4mm round, a flat opal, a 4mm round, a tube-shaped opal, a crystal, a flat opal, and a 4mm round. Repeat until the necklace is 1 in. (2.5cm) short of the desired length.

10 On the end of each wire, string a 3 x 2mm spacer, a crimp bead, and a spacer. Go through a loop on a two-strand clasp and back through the beads just strung. Tighten the wires, check the fit, and add or remove an equal number of beads on each strand if necessary. Crimp the crimp beads and trim the excess wire.

Combine fringed yarn and glass beads to make a lively necklace and hair accessory

by Rupa Balachandar

Blue is the most popular color in the western world. In these projects, blue partners with teal, green, blue-violet, and purple – the lively colors on a ceramic decanter – for an appealing palette that won't go out of style. For the dominant shades, use beads in deep aqua-blue and teal. For contrast, try using the strongest colors, purple and lime green, in small amounts, a trusted formula to follow for accents.

Green Blue

Although the beads appear to be strung directly onto the yarn, they're actually on a piece of beading wire. Wrap the yarn around the wire to create the braided effect.

materials

both projects
- Bernat boa yarn
- diagonal wire cutters

necklace 16 in. (41cm)
- 70–100 4–10mm glass and crystal beads, colors to match yarn
- 3g each size 8º and 11º seed beads
- 4 3mm round spacers
- 2 6–8mm bead caps
- box clasp
- flexible beading wire, .014 or .015
- 4 crimp beads
- chainnose or crimping pliers

ponytail holder
- 15–30 4–10mm glass and crystal beads, colors to match yarn
- 1g each size 8º and 11º seed beads
- 3½-in. (9cm) ponytail clip (Rio Grande, 800-545-6566, riogrande.com)
- 26- or 28-gauge craft wire
- Dritz Fray Check or clear nail polish

1 **necklace •** Determine the finished length of your necklace, (this one is 16 in./41cm), add 6 in. (15cm), and cut two pieces of beading wire to that length. On each wire, string assorted glass, crystal, and 8º and 11º seed beads until each strand is 1 in. (2.5cm) short of the desired length. Tape the ends.

3 On the two wires, string a bead cap, a round spacer, a crimp bead, a round spacer, and half the clasp. Go back through the beads just strung and tighten the wires. Crimp the crimp bead and trim the excess wire. Remove the tape from the other ends and re-tape the strands so the tape is flush against the last bead on each end.

editor's note

For ease in stringing boa yarn through a crimp bead, trim the yarn's fringe and apply clear nail polish or Dritz Fray Check to the end.

2 Cut a piece of boa yarn twice as long as the wire strands. Remove the tape from one end of each beaded strand. String the yarn and each beaded strand through a crimp bead. Crimp the crimp bead (see Basics, p. 8). Trim the excess yarn.

4 Wrap the yarn around each beaded strand, looping it around one strand, then the other. When you reach the last bead, remove the tape. Check the fit, and add or remove beads if necessary. String the wires and yarn through a crimp bead, crimp it, and trim the excess yarn. Attach the remaining clasp half as in step 3.

inspiration
decorative art

1 **ponytail holder •** Open the ponytail clip by squeezing it gently. Cut a 24-in. (61cm) piece of craft wire and a 30-in. (76cm) piece of boa yarn. Thread both through the hole at one end of the ponytail clip, leaving a 1-in. (2.5cm) tail. Twist the wire and yarn tails together and trim the excess.

2 Wrap the yarn around the ponytail clip. Wrap the wire around the clip and string a bead. Repeat across the clip, making sure to thread the wire under protruding parts of the clip.

3 After covering the clip with beads and yarn, twist the wire and yarn tails together. Trim the excess, apply a drop of Dritz Fray Check or nail polish to the yarn, and tuck the ends under a bead.

Blue Green

Peacock feathers play a starring role in a necklace and earring duo

by Jane Konkel

When you take your color cues from the blues and greens on a color wheel, it's hard to resist the sheer drama of adding peacock feathers to your design. Here, the feathers' saturated hues are combined with crystals and pearls in similar colors, keeping the focus on the feather while adding sparkle and texture to the finished jewelry.

inspiration
color wheel

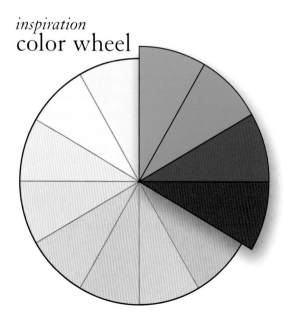

1 **necklace** • Trim the quill from a feather, leaving approximately ½ in. (1.3cm) at the top. String a 5mm bicone and a bead tip on the remaining quill, so the loop of the bead tip is at the top. Apply a dot of glue inside the bead tip and close it.

2 Measure the feather at its widest point and multiply that number by six. Cut a piece of 24-gauge wire to that length. Center a 6mm crystal on the wire. On each end, string a 5mm bicone, and two 4mm bicones.

There's nothing shy about a necklace and earrings that feature the sumptuous colors and dramatic flair of peacock feathers.

3 On each end, string an alternating pattern of 11º seed beads and keshi pearls, leaving 2 in. (5cm) of exposed wire. String ½ in. of 11ºs on each end. Shape the wire frame around the feather in an oval shape. Add or remove beads from each end, as desired.

4 Leaving ⅛ in. (3mm) of exposed wire on the stem, make a wrapped loop (see Basics, p. 8) at one end, bending it down as shown. Make a wrapped loop on the other end, bending it upward.

5 Wrap the tail of the top loop around the stem of the bottom loop, and the tail of the bottom around the stem of the top. Trim the excess wire.

6 Close the bead tip's loop around the bottom loop. Determine the finished length of your necklace. (This one is 15 in./38cm.) Add 6 in. (15cm) and cut a piece of flexible beading wire to that length. Open a 5mm jump ring (Basics) and connect it to the pendant's top loop. Close the jump ring. Center an 11º and the pendant on the wire. On each end, string a 4mm bicone and an 11º.

7 On each end, string an alternating pattern of five pearls and five 11ºs, followed by a 4mm bicone. Then string an alternating pattern of seven pearls and seven 11ºs and a 4mm bicone. Continue the pattern, increasing to nine pearls and 11ºs and a 4mm bicone, then to eleven pearls, and so on, until the necklace is 1 in. (2.5cm) short of the desired length. End with an 11º.

8 On one end, string a crimp bead, an 11º, and a jump ring with half of the clasp. Go back through the last beads strung. Repeat on the other end. Tighten the wires, check the fit, and add or remove an equal number of beads from each end if necessary. Crimp the crimp beads (Basics) and trim the excess wire.

materials

both projects
- chainnose pliers
- roundnose pliers
- diagonal wire cutters
- E6000 adhesive

necklace 15 in. (38cm)
- peacock feather
- 2 16-in. (41cm) strands 4–5mm keshi pearls, dark blue
- 2g size 11º seed or cylinder beads, gunmetal iris
- 6mm round crystal, Montana AB
- 3 5mm bicone crystals, olivine
- 14–18 4mm bicone crystals, topaz and smoked topaz AB
- box clasp
- 9–18 in. (23–46cm) 24-gauge wire, half-hard
- flexible beading wire, .014 or .015
- 2 crimp beads
- 3 5mm jump rings
- bead tip, clamshell style
- crimping pliers (optional)

earrings
- 2 peacock feathers
- 40–60 keshi pearls, dark blue
- 2g size 11º seed or cylinder beads, gunmetal iris
- 2 6mm round crystals, Montana AB
- 6 5mm bicone crystals, olivine
- 8 4mm bicone crystals, 4 smoked topaz AB and 4 Montana AB
- 12–24 in. (30–61cm) 24-gauge wire, half-hard
- 2 bead tips, clamshell style
- pair of earring wires

1 earrings • Follow steps 1–5 of the necklace. Close the bead tip's loop around the bottom loop.

2 Open an earring wire, attach the feather pendant, and close the earring wire. Make a second earring to match the first.

Blue

A necklace and earrings with faceted crystals recall the light-infused palette of a van Gogh painting

by Cheryl Phelan

In Vincent van Gogh's famous color studies, he experimented with bold contrasts; his painting *Vase with Lilacs, Daisies, and Anemones* is no exception. Here, high-key yellows create brilliant illumination when placed against a background dominated by intense blues and greens. When translating van Gogh's colors into jewelry, choose crystals in vivid colors and look for the way they turn on the lights.

inspiration fine art

Vase with Lilacs, Daisies, and Anemones by Vincent van Gogh, 1887. Oil on canvas.

1 necklace • String a 6mm blue cube crystal, a purple rondelle, and a 3mm blue bicone on a head pin, and make a plain loop (see Basics, p. 8) above the last bead. Make the following bead units the same way:
- 4mm blue cube, 5mm blue bicone, and 3mm blue (make one unit)
- 6mm green, 3mm blue (make one unit)
- 4mm green, 3mm blue (make two units)
- 3mm yellow, 3mm blue (make six units)
- 3mm green, 3mm blue (make four units)

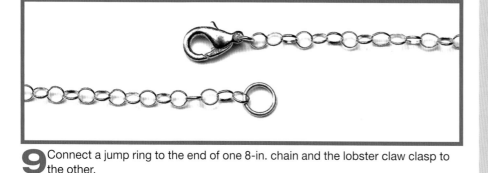

2 Cut a 1¾-in. (4.4cm) piece of wire and make a plain loop at one end. String an end link of a seven-link piece of cable chain, a 3mm blue bicone, a 6mm blue cube, a 4mm dark blue bicone, a blue bicone/cube unit, a 4mm dark blue bicone, a 6mm blue cube, a 3mm blue bicone, and a seven-link piece of chain. Make a plain loop next to the chain.

3 Cut a 1½-in. (3.8cm) piece of wire and make a plain loop at one end. String a 3mm blue bicone, a 4mm blue cube, a 4mm dark blue bicone, a purple rondelle/cube unit, a 4mm dark blue bicone, a 4mm blue cube, and a 3mm blue bicone. Make a loop next to the end bead.

4 Open the loops (Basics) on the component made in step 3 and attach each end chain link on the component made in step 2. Attach an 11-link chain to each loop. Close the loops.

5 Connect the end links of the 11-link chains with a 6mm green/3mm blue unit.

6 Cut two 8-in. (20cm) pieces of chain. Open the loops on the upper component and attach an end link of each chain to each loop. Close the loops.

7 Skip a link next to the bottom unit and connect a 3mm yellow/blue unit. Skip a link and connect a 3mm green/blue unit. Repeat, connecting five units to each 11-link chain, alternating colors as shown.

8 Connect a 4mm green/3mm blue unit to each loop on the upper component.

9 Connect a jump ring to the end of one 8-in. chain and the lobster claw clasp to the other.

materials

both projects
- roundnose pliers
- chainnose pliers
- diagonal wire cutters

necklace 17 in. (43cm)
- 6mm faceted rondelle crystal, purple
- 6mm bicone crystal, green
- 5mm bicone crystal, blue
- 4mm bicone crystals
  4 dark blue
  2 green
- 3mm bicone crystals
  19 blue
  6 yellow
  4 green
- cube crystals, diagonal hole
  3 6mm blue
  3 4mm blue
- 4 in. (10cm) 22-gauge wire
- 20 in. (51cm) 3.5mm cable chain
- 15 1-in. (2.5cm) head pins
- lobster claw clasp with jump ring

earrings
- 6mm bicone crystals
  2 green
  2 purple
- 4 4mm cube crystals, diagonal hole, blue
- 3mm bicone crystals
  36 blue
  16 green
  16 yellow
- 2 in. (5cm) 22-gauge wire
- 2 in. (5cm) 3.5mm cable chain
- 5 in. (13cm) 2mm cable chain
- 36 1-in. (2.5cm) head pins
- pair of earring wires

1 earrings • String the following pairs of bicone crystals on head pins and make a plain loop above the top bead on each unit:

- 3mm green, 3mm blue (make 16 units)
- 3mm yellow, 3mm blue (make 16 units)
- 6mm green, 3mm blue (make two units)
- 6mm purple, 3mm blue (make two units)

Set half of each type of unit aside for the second earring.

2 Cut a 1-in. (2.5cm) piece of wire. Make a plain loop at one end, string a 4mm cube, a four-link piece of 2mm cable chain, and a 4mm cube. Make a second loop in the same plane as the first. Open the loops and connect a 15-link piece of 2mm cable chain to each one. Don't close the loops.

3 Cut a nine-link piece of 3.5mm cable chain and attach an end link to each loop. Close the loops. Open the loop on a 6mm purple/ 3mm blue unit and connect it to the short center chain. Close the loop.

4 Connect the end links of the long chains with a 6mm green/3mm blue unit.

5 Connect 3mm units to every other chain link on each side (a total of 14) as in step 7 of the necklace.

6 Connect a 3mm green/ blue unit to the loops made in step 2.

7 Slide an earring wire into the middle chain link. Use the remaining units from step 1 to make a second earring to match the first.

Blue

Shades of blue merge in two luscious multistrand necklaces

by Naomi Fujimoto

This sky blue vase with its violet base pairs two lovely, cool jewel tones. In this necklace, a rich purple iolite pendant and amethyst-colored crystals add depth and definition to layers of transparent blue beads. A second version (page 60) makes a bolder statement. Four shades of blue beads, both smooth and faceted, dominate the piece, but a blue-violet strand of lavender jade adds subtle contrast, and a strand of silvery pearls lightens the dark composition.

Keep your versions of the multistrand necklaces relatively short. They're designed to be worn right at the collarbone.

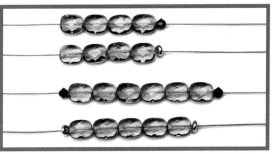

1 **necklace with pendant •**
Determine the finished length of the shortest strand (this one is 15 in./38cm), add 6 in. (15cm), and cut a piece of beading wire to that length. Cut five more strands, each 1 in. (2.5cm) longer than the previous one. On the shortest wire, center a spacer. String six rectangles and a spacer on each end. Repeat until the strand is 2 in. (5cm) short of the desired length.

2 String the next four strands until each is 2 in. short of the desired length:
- **Strand 2:** String four rectangles and a crystal. Repeat.
- **Strand 3:** String four rectangles and a spacer. Repeat.
- **Strand 4:** Center a crystal. String six rectangles and a crystal on each end. Repeat.
- **Strand 5:** Center a spacer. String five rectangles and a spacer on each end. Repeat.

3 Center the briolette on the longest strand. String a crystal and five rectangles on each end. Repeat until the strand is 2 in. short of the desired length.

4 Cut two 4-in. (10cm) pieces of 22-gauge wire. At one end of each wire, make a wrapped loop (see Basics, p. 8) slightly larger than the hole at the small end of the cone.

On one end of each strand, string approximately ½ in. (1.3cm) of 11º seed beads, a crimp bead, an 11º, and the wire loop. Go back through the 11º, the crimp bead, and two 11ºs. Tighten the wire. Repeat at the other end of the necklace. Repeat for the remaining strands.

inspiration
decorative art

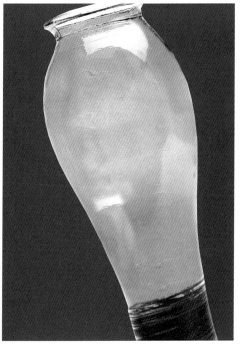

5 Check the fit, allowing 1½ in. (3.8cm) for finishing. Add or remove an equal number of beads from each end, if necessary. Crimp the crimp beads (Basics) and trim the excess wire.

6 On one end, string a cone and a crystal on the wire. Make the first half of a wrapped loop above the crystal. Repeat at the other end.

7 On each end, attach half the clasp to the loop. Complete the wraps.

1 **mixed-bead necklace** • Determine the finished length of the shortest strand (this one is 13½ in./34.3cm), add 6 in. (15cm), and cut a piece of beading wire to that length. Cut five more strands, each 1 in. (2.5cm) longer than the previous one.

2 String beads on each wire until each one is 2 in. (5cm) short of the desired length. Finish the necklace as in steps 4–8 of the pendant necklace.

materials

both necklaces
- flexible beading wire, .014 or .015
- chainnose pliers
- roundnose pliers
- diagonal wire cutters
- crimping pliers (optional)

pendant necklace
15 in. (38cm)
- 14 x 17mm briolette, iolite
- 6 16-in. (41cm) strands
  7 x 9mm faceted glass rectangles, blue

- 30–40 4mm bicone crystals, amethyst
- 1g size 11º seed beads, blue
- 25–35 3–4mm flat spacers
- 2 12 x 19mm cones
- toggle clasp
- 8 in. (20cm) 22-gauge wire
- 12 crimp beads

mixed bead necklace
13½ in. (34cm)
- 16-in. strand each of the following:
  10mm round beads, blueberry quartz

8mm round shell beads, blue
6mm round pearls, silver
5–6mm button-shaped pearls, dark blue
4mm round beads, lavender jade
3–4mm chalcedony rondelles
- 2 4mm crystals
- 1g size 11º seed beads
- 2 12 x 19mm cones
- toggle clasp
- 8 in. 22-gauge wire
- 12 crimp beads

Enjoy this beaded chain in one of several necklace styles or as a stylish belt.

Blue

A versatile necklace doubles as a chain belt

By Naomi Fujimoto

inspiration fabric

Vivid splashes of red, orange, yellow, and aqua dance across the predominantly dark blue hues of this whimsical fabric. For this jewelry, replace the fabric's yellow and orange with gold chain and pearls, and work with beads in red, pink, aqua, and blue. Although shown on page 63 on white trousers, this piece will also stand out against a dark blue shirt or indigo jeans.

full-length necklace

two-strand
necklace

materials

both projects
- chainnose pliers
- roundnose pliers
- diagonal wire cutters

belt/necklace 36 in. (.9m)
- 20–30 8mm round crystals, in 2 colors
- 8–10 8mm faceted round gemstones beads, in 2 colors
- 7–10 8mm round pearls
- 35–50 3–4mm flat spacers
- 40–60 in. (1–1.5m) cable or long-and-short chain, 4–5mm links
- lobster claw clasp
- 40–60 1½-in. (3.8cm) head pins
- 4–5mm jump ring

earrings
- 2 8mm round crystals
- 2 3–4mm flat spacers
- 1–2 in. (2.5–5cm) cable or long-and-short chain, 4–5mm links
- 2 1½-in. (3.8cm) head pins
- pair of earring wires

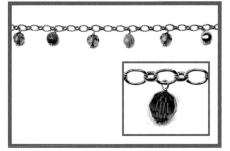

1 **belt/necklace •** To make the dangles, string a spacer and an 8mm bead on a head pin. Make the first half of a wrapped loop (see Basics, p. 8) above the bead. Make a total of 40–50 dangles: 20–25 with crystals, ten or more with gemstones, and ten or more with pearls.

2 Determine the desired finished length of your belt by wrapping a piece of chain around your waist. Add 8–10 in. (20–25cm) for the extender and cut the chain to that length. (This belt is 1 yd./.9m, plus an 8-in. extender.) Attach the clasp to the chain's end link with a jump ring (Basics).

3 Attach a crystal dangle to the third or fourth chain link from the clasp. Finish the wraps. Attach a dangle to every third or fourth link, alternating gemstone and pearl dangles with crystal dangles, until the beaded section fits around your waist. Do not attach dangles to the remaining chain (the extender).

4 Check the fit and trim the chain if the extender is too long. Attach a dangle to the end link and finish the wraps.

editor's tip

To make the belt wearable as a choker, determine the finished length by wrapping the chain around your neck three times. Then wrap the chain around your waist or hips. The chain should fit comfortably, with 8–10 in. left over for an extender.

1 **earrings •** Make a dangle as in step 1 of the necklace.

2 Cut a ½–1-in. (1.3–2.5cm) piece of chain. Attach the dangle to an end link and finish the wraps.

3 Open the loop on an earring wire and attach the dangle. Close the loop. Make a second earring to match the first.

fashionable belt

Glass, gemstone, pearl, and enamel beads provide different tones and finishes for this jewelry set.

Indigo

Pairing dark and light shades creates a dramatic necklace and earrings set

by Helene Tsigistras

inspiration
color wheel

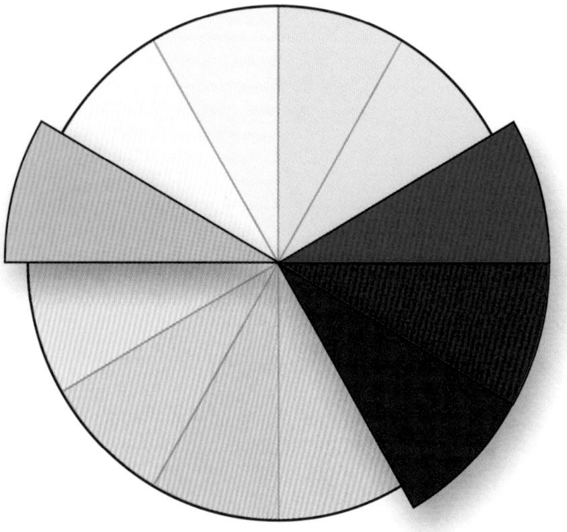

This striking ensemble uses an analogous color scheme – blue, indigo, and violet – with indigo's complement, yellow-orange, for contrast. The drama is heightened by the use of different color values. Deep indigo and violet tones leap out against the lightest yellow-orange and blue. The result is playful, yet sophisticated.

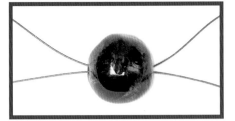

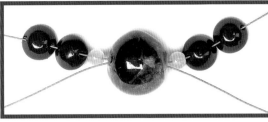

1 **necklace** • Determine the finished length of your necklace (this one is 18½ in./47cm), add six in. (15cm), and cut two strands of flexible beading wire to that length. Center the art bead on both strands.

2 On one wire, string a 5mm gemstone and two button beads on each side of the art bead.

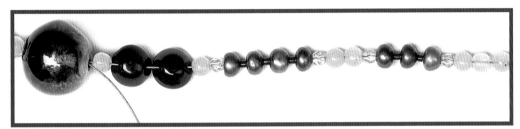

3 On both ends of the wire, string a gemstone, a 3mm fire-polished bead, and an alternating pattern of four pearls and three 11° seed beads. String a 3mm, two gemstones, a 3mm, and an alternating pattern of three pearls and two seed beads.

String a 3mm, three gemstones, and continue the pattern, alternating between three- and four-pearl segments, and two- and three-gemstone segments, as shown, until the necklace is within 1 in. (2.5cm) of the desired length.

4 On each end of the other wire, string a 3mm, a pearl, a seed bead, a pearl, a 3mm, a gemstone, a 3mm, a pearl, a seed bead, a pearl, a 3mm, and three button beads on each side. Repeat the pattern until the necklace is within 1 in. of the desired length, alternating three- and two-button groups.

5 String a crimp bead and the loop of a clasp half on both wires at one end. Go back through the crimp bead and tighten the wire so the button beads nestle together. Repeat at the other end of the necklace. Check the fit. The button-bead strand should sit outside the other strand. Add or remove beads from both ends as necessary. Crimp the crimp beads (see Basics, p. 8), and trim the tails.

1 **earrings** • String a pearl on a head pin and make a wrapped loop (Basics). Make three more pearl units.

2 String a button bead, a 3mm, and a gemstone on a head pin. Make the first half of a wrapped loop above the beads.

3 Attach two of the pearl units to the button bead unit and complete the wraps.

4 Open the loop on an ear wire. Attach a pearl unit, the button bead unit, and a pearl unit. Close the loops. Make a second earring to match the first.

Knots made with consistent tension form a precise spiral. Embellish your macramé with spacers or other large-hole beads.

A macramé necklace interspersed with silver beads supports an opal pendant

by Debbie Nishihara

inspiration nature

Indigo

What better way to re-enact the magic of a Blue Morpho's wings than with opal? The stunning characteristic of both is iridescence: color created by the reflection and refraction of light. Here, a boulder opal paired with indigo-colored cord picks up the deep blues that define the butterfly's silhouette, and frayed cord ends echo the motif of fluttering wings.

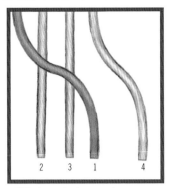

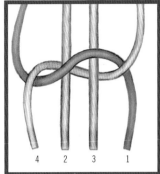

1 Cut two 50-in. (1.3m) and two 30-in. (76cm) lengths of cord to make an 18-in. (46cm) necklace. Gather four ends together and bring the cords through the loop on half the clasp. Slide the clasp to 8-in. (20cm) from one set of cut ends. Tie all the cords together with a double overhand knot (see Basics, p. 8). Slide a spacer over the four long cords and next to the knot.

2 Attach the cords to a workboard by placing T-pins through the clasp loop. Arrange the working cords in a row so the two shortest are in the middle. Number the cords from left to right. Bring cord 1 over cords 2 and 3.

3 Bring cord 4 over cord 1, under cords 3 and 2, and up through the hole created by cord 1. Pull the outer cords tight to move the knot up to the spacer.

4 Renumber the cords 1–4 after every knot. Continue knotting from the left so the knots create a spiral. Make ½ in. (1.3cm) of knots. String two spacers over all four cords and slide them up against the knots.

5 Knot for 1¼ in. (3.2cm). String an accent bead over all four cords and slide it against the knots. Repeat until you have strung a total of three accent beads. Keep your knots tight against the accent beads.

6 Knot for 1½ in. (3.8cm) and string a spacer over all four cords. Knot for ½ in. and string two spacers. Knot for 1½ in. and string a spacer bead. String the opal focal bead over all four cords and slide it against the last spacer. Check the fit and adjust the length, if necessary, by adding or removing knots before the opal and spacer.

7 Position the opal at the top of your workboard and secure with T-pins. Make the second half of the necklace to mirror the first.

8 Slide the remaining clasp half over all four cords and tie a double overhand knot around the clasp loop. On each tail, string a fire-polished bead and two 8° seed beads. Vary the position of the beads and tie a double overhand knot on each tail.

9 Dot all the overhand knots, including those attaching the clasp, with glue and let dry. Trim the tails to 1 in. (2.5cm) past the knots, and fray the ends by rubbing the cords back and forth between your thumb and index finger.

materials

necklace 18 in. (46cm)
- boulder opal focal bead (Eclectica, 262-641-0910 or Opal Illusions, 707-699-7887)
- 6 13mm silver accent beads (Fire Mountain Gems, 800-355-2137, firemountaingems.com)
- 14 7mm star-shaped spacers
- 8 4mm faceted round fire-polished beads, blue
- 16 8° seed beads, dark blue
- box clasp (Jess Imports, jessimports.com)
- Tuff cord, size 3, navy (Shor International, shorinternational.com)
- G-S Hypo Cement
- macramé workboard
- T-pins

Violet

Enhance the regal hues of amethyst gemstones with crystal accents

by Debbie Nishihara

The unexpected addition of aqua crystals adds pizzazz to this classic necklace.

inspiration
color wheel

Faceted amethysts take on a lively, contemporary feel when aqua crystals are their companions. This unusual pairing works because the violet of the amethysts and green-blue of the crystals form half of a reliably compatible foursome on the color wheel known as a tetrad, which also includes their complements, yellow and red-orange, respectively.

materials

necklace 20 in. (51cm)

- amethyst pendant (Eclectica, 262-641-0910)
- **16** 12mm silver bead clusters (Fire Mountain Gems, 800-355-2137, firemountaingems.com)
- amethyst beads
  20 8mm round faceted
  22 6mm round faceted
- **32** 4mm bicone crystals
- seed beads
  2 size 6º, any color
  8 size 8º, purple
- flat spacers
  4 6mm
  54 4mm
- toggle clasp
- flexible beading wire, .014
- **2** crimp beads
- crimping pliers
- diagonal wire cutters

editor's tip

The silver bead clusters are cast elements with a distinct front and back. You can substitute other small charms for the clusters, if desired.

1 Determine the finished length of your necklace (this one is 20 in./51cm), add 6 in. (15cm), and cut a piece of beading wire to that length. Center the pendant on the wire.

2 String two 6º seed beads, an 8mm amethyst, a 6mm spacer, and an 8mm amethyst next to the pendant. Slide the pendant's bail over the 6ºs.

3 On the other side of the pendant, string an 8mm amethyst, a 6mm spacer, and an 8mm amethyst.

4 On each end, string a 4mm spacer, a bicone crystal, a silver bead cluster, a bicone, and a 4mm spacer. String this pattern seven times on each end, with an 8mm amethyst between each repetition. End with a 4mm spacer.

5 String an 8mm amethyst and a 6mm spacer. Then string a repeating pattern of 6mm amethysts and 4mm spacers until you've strung a total of 11 6mm amethysts. End with a 4mm spacer. Repeat at the other end.

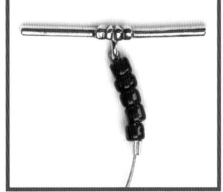

6 Check the fit, and add or remove beads if necessary. On one end, string an 8º, a crimp bead, and five 8ºs. Go through the loop on the toggle bar and back through the 8ºs, the crimp bead, and the next few beads. Tighten the wire and crimp the crimp bead (see Basics, p. 8). Trim the excess wire.

7 On the other end, string an 8º, a crimp bead, and an 8º. Go through the loop on the other clasp section and back through the 8º, the crimp bead, and the 8º. Tighten the wire, allowing for some flexibility, and crimp the crimp bead. Trim the excess wire.

Bead colors, shapes, sizes, and finishes work in complete harmony in this striking bracelet design.

Violet

Add texture to a multistrand bracelet with a mix of faceted and smooth beads

inspiration nature

by Cheryl Phelan

The evening sky is one of nature's most dramatic palettes. To capture the range of twilight colors, choose beads in purples, blues, and pinks as dominant colors, then add two complements, yellow and orange, for bright contrast. On each strand, colors progress from dark to light, but staggering the pattern creates a sense of movement in the diagonal bands of color.

materials

bracelet 7 in. (18cm)
- Czech fire-polished beads
  19 6mm purple
  5 6mm dark blue
  8 3mm bright pink
- 10 6mm faceted round glass beads, violet
- 10 6mm cube-shaped glass beads, purple
- 10 6mm triangle-shaped glass beads, orange
- faceted rondelles
  20–24 6mm purple
  10 6mm yellow
  10 4mm opaque pink
- 10–15 4mm square glass beads, purple
- 20 4mm round glass beads, orange
- 110–120 3mm disk-shaped glass beads, pink, violet, and purple
- five-strand slide clasp
- flexible beading wire, .014
- 10 crimp beads
- 10 crimp covers (optional)
- chainnose pliers
- crimping pliers
- diagonal wire cutters

1 Determine the finished length of your bracelet, add 5 in. (13cm), and cut five strands of beading wire to that length. Set four strands aside.

2 Center a blue 6mm fire-polished bead on one wire. On each end, string a disk, a 6mm cube, a disk, a purple 6mm fire-polished bead, a disk, a 4mm square, a disk, a 6mm faceted round, and a disk.

3 On each end, string a purple 6mm rondelle, a disk, a 4mm rondelle, a disk, a purple 6mm rondelle, a disk, a 6mm triangle, a 4mm round, a yellow 6mm rondelle, a 4mm round, disk, a 6mm triangle, a disk, a 3mm fire-polished bead, a disk, a purple 6mm fire-polished bead, and a disk. Use this as the center strand. Tape the ends to your beading surface.

4 On a second strand of beading wire, string the pattern in step 2. Position the second strand under the first, aligning the blue fire-polished bead under a 6mm cube. String the bead sequence in step 3. On one end, you'll need to cut the pattern short; on the other end, you'll continue the pattern for a few more beads. Tape this strand in place when it is the same length as the first.

5 Repeat step 4 for the third strand.

6 Repeat steps 4 and 5, positioning the strands above the center strand, as shown.

7 At one end, string a crimp bead on each wire, go through the corresponding loop on a five-strand clasp, and back through the crimp bead and a few more beads. Repeat at the other end.

8 Check the fit, and add or remove beads from one end if necessary. Make sure the strands are the same length. Crimp the crimp beads (see Basics, p. 8) and trim the excess wire.

9 Cover each crimp bead with a crimp cover, if desired.

Violet

Weave shell and gemstone beads together for a vibrant necklace, bracelet, and earrings set

by Helene Tsigistras

Vibrant red-violet takes center stage in this unusual split-complementary color scheme inspired by a shimmering satin fabric. The dyed shell beads imitate the iridescent nature of the violet backdrop, while the red-orange and green gemstones mimic the eye-catching beauty of the butterfly wings. The regal pattern of the beads is easy to achieve with a simple two-strand weave.

inspiration fabric

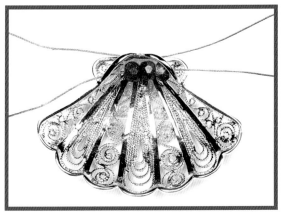

1 **necklace •** Determine the finished length of your necklace (this one is 19½ in./49.5cm), add 12 in. (30cm), and cut two strands of flexible beading wire to that length. Center the pendant unit on the strands, stringing rondelles within the pendant to support it.

2 On one side of the pendant, string two rondelles and a size 15º seed bead on each wire, then cross the wires through a gemstone bead.

3 String a seed bead and two rondelles on each wire. Pass each wire through a hole on a double-drilled shell bead.

4 Repeat steps 2 and 3 on the other end of the necklace. Continue the pattern on both sides until the necklace is within 1½ in. (3.8cm) of the desired length.

Although these woven strands look complicated, you can create them easily with a simple two-strand weave.

5 On one end of the necklace, string a crimp bead and the loop on a clasp half on each wire. Go back through the crimp beads and tighten the wires. Repeat on the other end of the necklace, making sure all the beads are snug and orderly. Check the fit, add or remove beads from both ends as necessary, and crimp the crimp beads (see Basics, p. 8). Trim the tails.

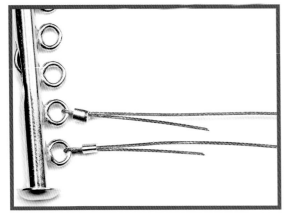

1 **bracelet** • Determine the finished length of your bracelet (this one is 7½ in./19.1cm), add 6 in. (15cm), and cut five pieces of flexible beading wire to that length. String a crimp bead on one strand and go through the bottom loop on a clasp half. Go back through the crimp bead and crimp. Repeat with another crimp bead and wire strand on the second loop.

2 On each wire, string a rondelle and one hole of a double-drilled shell.

3 On each wire, string two rondelles and a seed bead. Cross the wires through a gemstone bead. String a seed bead, two rondelles, and one hole of a shell bead on each wire.

4 Repeat step 3 until the strand is within 1 in. (2.5cm) of the desired length. Tape the ends to secure.

5 Attach a strand of beading wire to each of the loops on the other end of the clasp half. Repeat steps 2–4 to create a matching pattern with these strands.

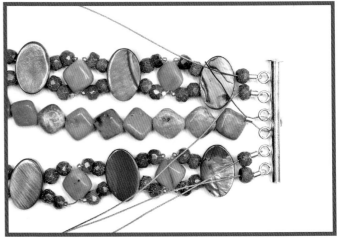

6 String a crimp bead and the remaining loop(s) of the clasp half. Go back through the crimp bead and crimp. String gemstones until the strand is within 1 in. of the desired length.

7 Untape the ends of the wires. String a crimp bead on each wire and take the strand through the corresponding loop on the other clasp half. Go back through the crimp beads. Tighten the wires so the pattern is snug and crimp the crimp beads. Trim the wire tails.

1 **earrings •** Cut a 6 in. (15cm) length of flexible beading wire. String one hole of a double-drilled shell bead on each end.

2 String three rondelles and an 11º on each end, and cross the wires through a gemstone bead.

3 String an 11º and three rondelles on each strand, then string a rondelle and a crimp over both wires.

4 Tighten the wires and go back through the crimp bead. Use your roundnose pliers to hold the loop in place and pull the wire tight. Crimp the crimp bead and trim the tails.

Open the loop (Basics) on an earwire and attach the earring. Close the loop. Make a second earring to match the first.

materials

all projects
- chainnose pliers
- roundnose pliers
- diagonal wire cutters
- crimping pliers

necklace 19½ in. (50cm)
- 30 x 45mm filigree pendant
- 18 15 x 10mm double-drilled oval shell beads, violet
- 18 9mm diamond-shaped gemstones, green turquoise
- 2 16-in. strands 3mm rondelles, sunstone

- 3g size 15º seed beads, silver-plated
- toggle clasp
- flexible beading wire, .012–.015
- 4 crimp beads

bracelet 7½ in. (19cm)
- 14 15 x 10mm double-drilled oval shell beads, violet
- 16-in. strand 9mm diamond-shaped gemstones, green turquoise
- 2 16-in. strands 3mm rondelles, sunstone
- 3g size 15º seed beads, silver-plated
- flexible beading wire, .012–.015

- 10 crimp beads
- five-strand slide clasp

earrings
- 2 15 x 10mm double-drilled oval shell beads, violet
- 2 9mm diamond-shaped gemstones, green turquoise
- 13 3mm rondelles, sunstone
- 8 size 150 seed beads, silver-plated
- flexible beading wire, .012–.015
- 2 crimp beads
- pair earring wires

Brown

A blend of subtle hues captures the soft tones of a favorite shell in a multistrand necklace

by Katee Lee Chimpouras

To create this variegated palette, mix beads in several colors and finishes in a small bowl before you string them.

Satin-finished beads in colors ranging from feathery grays to beige to soft peach do an excellent impersonation of the weathered texture and faded color of seashells. Crystals in varying shapes and sizes contrast gently with the monochromatic tones without disturbing the overall sense of unity. The finished piece looks as if it could have washed ashore alongside the shells it imitates.

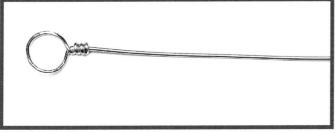

1 Cut four 6-in. (15cm) pieces of 20-gauge wire. Use the largest part of your roundnose pliers to make a 5mm or larger wrapped loop (see Basics, p. 8) at one end of each wire.

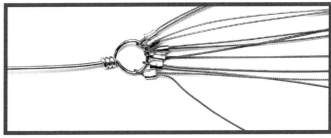

2 Determine the finished length of your necklace. (This one is 18 in./46cm.) Double that measurement, add 8 in. (20cm), and cut 13 pieces of flexible beading wire to that length.

3 Center one piece of beading wire on a wire loop, slide a crimp bead over both ends, and slide the crimp bead close to the loop. Crimp the crimp bead (Basics). Make a total of six crimped pairs on one loop.

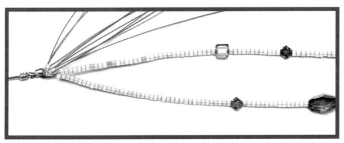

4 String 2½ in. (6.4cm) of Japanese cylinder beads, then string a 2½-in. section of cylinder beads interspersed with crystals. Alternate these sections, ending with a cylinder bead section, until the strand is 3 in. (7.6cm) short of the desired length. Repeat on the remaining strands; if desired, string four or five strands using only cylinder beads.

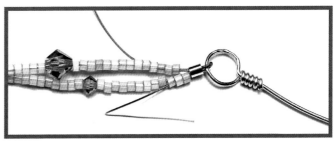

5 Check the fit, allowing 3 in. for the cones and clasp. Add or remove beads from each wire to even the ends. Working in pairs, string a crimp bead over both wires, go through a wire loop from step 1, and go back through the crimp bead. Separate the wires and pass each through a few beads. Crimp the crimp beads and trim the excess wire. Repeat with each pair.

6 Repeat steps 3 through 5 with the remaining wire loops and seven strands of beading wire. Place one beaded section over the other. Wrap one wire stem around the other, as if making a wrapped loop. Trim the excess wrapping wire. Repeat on the other end.

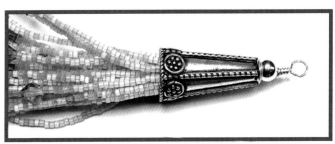

7 String a cone and a 6mm bead on the wire. Pull the wire and beads snugly into the cone. Make a wrapped loop above the bead, continuing the wraps until they reach the 6mm bead. Trim the excess wire. Repeat on the other end.

materials

necklace 18 in. (46cm)
- 125–175 3–8mm crystals, assorted shapes, colors
- 2 6mm beads
- 35–40g Japanese cylinder beads, satin finish
- 2 25mm cones with a 12mm opening
- lobster claw or S-hook clasp and 2 jump rings

- flexible beading wire, .012–.014
- 2 ft. (61cm) 20-gauge silver wire, half-hard
- 26 crimp beads
- chainnose pliers
- roundnose pliers
- crimping pliers
- diagonal wire cutters

8 Use a jump ring to attach a lobster claw clasp to either loop, or attach an S-hook clasp. Attach a second jump ring to the remaining loop, if desired.

Brown

Mix rich shades of browns and golds in a two-strand necklace

by Cheryl Phelan

The muted earthtone vines on a paper-covered box are reminiscent of faded country designs found on old, varnished furniture. This necklace captures the warmth of a traditional palette with a combination of opaque and translucent beads in a range of browns and golds. Light passing through the gemstones keeps the composition from becoming too somber.

The etched pendant rests on a seed bead centered on the bottom strand.

1 Center an 11º seed bead on an 18-in. (46cm) length of Fireline. Hold the ends together and string the focal bead over both ends. Slide it next to the 11º.

2 Thread both ends through a twisted-wire needle. String a 4mm dark brown wood bead and an 11º five times.

3 Go back through the first 4mm and the focal bead to form a loop. Then go through the 11º and the focal bead again. Secure the beads by tying half-hitch knots (see Basics, p. 8) between a few beads in the loop. Glue the last knot and trim the excess Fireline.

4 Determine the finished length of the pendant strand, which is the lower strand of the necklace. (This one is 18 in.) Add 6 in. (15cm) and cut two pieces of beading wire to that length. On one wire, string a 4mm tan bead, the focal bead's loop, an 11º, and a 4mm tan.

5 Position the focal bead's loop over the 11º. On one side, string a 10mm round, a rondelle, a 10mm, and a 4mm tan. Repeat on the other side of the pendant.

6 Continue stringing this pattern on both ends until you are 1 in. (2.5cm) short of the desired length.

materials

necklace 18 in. (46cm)

- 30–35mm focal bead, pietersite
- 16-in. (41cm) strands of gemstone beads:
  10mm round Botswana agate
  8mm Labradorite rondelles
- 16-in. strands 4mm wood beads, **1** each dark brown and tan

- 2g size 11º seed beads, gray
- two-strand clasp
- flexible beading wire, .012-.014
- Fireline 6–8-lb. test
- 4 crimp beads
- twisted-wire needles
- diagonal wire cutters
- crimping pliers

inspiration
decorative art

7 On the other wire, string an 11º, five 4mm dark browns, an 11º, and a 4mm tan. Repeat this pattern until the strand is 1 in. shorter than the first strand.

8 String a crimp bead and half the clasp on one end of the longer strand. Go back through the last beads strung. Repeat with the shorter strand, then repeat with the other ends. Check the fit, and add or remove beads if necessary. Crimp the crimp beads (Basics) and trim the excess wire.

Brown

Combine the earthy colors of autumn in a classic necklace and earrings duo

by Jane Konkel

Browns and greens are a winning combination in nature as well as manmade applications. Take a cue from a home-decorating fabric, and use copper chain as a background color for dangling leaf-shaped beads in alternating green and amber tones. A second strand with larger leaves in burnt orange and an intrepid yellow bead in the center is the perfect accent to cap off the necklace with flair.

inspiration fabric

Pressed-glass leaves add movement and interest to a multistrand chain necklace.

1 **necklace** • To make the pendant, cut a 1½-in. (3.8cm) piece of 22-gauge wire. Make a plain loop (see Basics, p. 8) at one end. String the 18 x 35mm leaf-shaped bead and make a plain loop. Repeat with the 12 x 16mm leaves.

2 Open a loop (Basics) on the 35mm leaf, attach one loop of a 12 x 16mm leaf, and close the loop. Repeat with the other 12 x 16mm leaf.

3 Cut four 2½-in. (6.4cm) pieces of wire. Make the first half of a wrapped loop (Basics) on each. On two of the wires, string a bicone crystal, a spacer, a rondelle, a spacer, and a crystal. Make the first half of a wrapped loop. On the other two wires, string a fire-polished bead, a spacer, a rondelle, a spacer, and a fire-polished bead. Make the first half of a wrapped loop.

4 For the necklace sides, cut four 2½-in. and two 1¾-in. (4.4cm) pieces of 6mm chain. Connect a jump ring and a 2½-in. piece of chain to each of the 12 x 16mm leaves.

5 Connect a fire-polished bead unit to one 2½-in. chain. Connect a 1¾-in. chain to its other loop. Finish the wraps. Connect a bicone bead unit to the end chain link. Connect a 2½-in. chain to the other loop. Finish the wraps. Repeat on the other side of the pendant.

6 Determine the finished length of your necklace's shorter chain. (This one is 15 in./38cm.) Cut a piece of 3mm chain to that length. Find the center link of the chain. Open a jump ring, attach a 5 x 9mm leaf to the center link, and close the jump ring. Attach a leaf bead to every other link in the chain, alternating colors.

7 Check the fit, and trim an equal number of links from each end if necessary. Open a jump ring and attach the links at one end of the chains to a clasp half. Close the jump ring. Repeat on the other end.

1 **earrings •** Cut a 2¼-in. (5.7cm) piece of 3mm chain. Find the center link of the chain. Open a jump ring, attach a leaf dangle to the center link, and close the jump ring. Attach the remaining dangles to every other link, alternating colors.

2 Cut a 2½-in. (6.4cm) piece of wire. Make the first half of a wrapped loop. String a fire-polished bead, a spacer, a rondelle, a spacer, and a fire-polished bead. Make the first half of a wrapped loop.

3 Attach both ends of the chain to one loop on the bead unit. Complete both wrapped loops.

4 Open the loop on an earring wire, attach the dangle, and close the loop. Make a second earring to match the first.

materials

both projects
- chainnose pliers
- roundnose pliers
- diagonal wire cutters

necklace 15 in. (38cm)
- 18 x 35mm leaf-shaped bead (Fire Mountain Gems, 800-355-2137, firemountaingems.com)
- 2 12 x 16mm leaf-shaped beads (Fire Mountain Gems)
- 39 or more 5 x 9mm leaf-shaped beads in 2 colors (Eclectica, 262-641-0910)

- 4 8mm faceted glass rondelles in 2 colors
- 4 4mm fire-polished beads
- 4 4mm bicone crystals
- 8 5mm flat spacers
- 14 in. (36cm) antiqued-copper chain, 6mm links (Ornamentea, 919-834-8634, ornamentea.com)
- antiqued copper toggle clasp
- 15 in. (38cm) antiqued-copper chain, 3mm links
- 12½ in. (31.8cm) 22-gauge copper-plated wire
- 43 5mm copper-plated jump rings

earrings
- 18 5 x 9mm leaf-shaped beads in 2 colors (Eclectica)
- 2 8mm faceted glass rondelles
- 4 4mm fire-polished beads
- 4 5mm flat spacers
- 4½ in. (11.4cm) antiqued-copper chain, 3mm links
- 5 in. (13cm) 22-gauge copper-plated wire
- 18 5mm copper-plated jump rings
- pair of copper-plated leverback earring wires

Metallic Bronze

Blend warm shades of gold with deeper tones of bronze and orange for a lustrous jewelry set

by Helene Tsigistras

The metallic gleam and rich colors of this decorative plate offer plenty of inspiration for gorgeous jewelry in shades of bronze, gold, and brown. Pearls offer the right amount of luster in metallic tones, while the carnelian beads add a spark of drama to the set. The blended shades of the plate, reminiscent of gold-leaf, are matched by the organic shapes of the pearls.

inspiration
decorative art

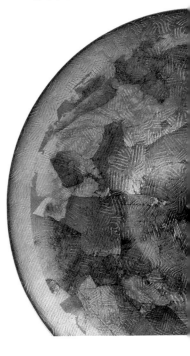

The enamel clasp on this necklace matches the pendant.

1 **necklace •** Cut a 2½-in. (6.4cm) length of wire and make a plain loop (see Basics, p. 8) at one end. String a spacer, a rondelle, a spacer, a rondelle, the pendant, a spacer, a rondelle, a spacer, and a rondelle.

2 Pull the beads tight against the loop and curve the wire into a circle. Pull the tail through the loop and twist the wire around itself, as in a wrapped loop (Basics). Trim the excess wire.

3 String a rondelle on a head pin and make the first half of a wrapped loop. Make a total of five rondelle dangles. Cut a ½-in. (1.3cm) piece of chain (this one is three links long). Attach a dangle to the bottom link of chain and complete the wraps.

4 Attach the remaining dangles to the chain, and complete the wraps. Make sure the dangles sit evenly on either side of the chain, as shown.

5 Open a jump ring (Basics), and string the end link of the chain. Attach the jump ring to the pendant ring, so that the chain unit hangs in front of the pendant.

6 Cut a 2-in. (5cm) length of wire and make a plain loop at one end. Alternate stringing rondelles and spacers until you have six beads. Repeat step 2 to finish the bead ring. Make a total of four bead rings.

7 Determine the finished length of your necklace (this one is 16 in./41cm), add six in. (15cm), and cut two strands of flexible beading wire to that length. Center the pendant unit and a spacer over both strands.

8 On one wire, string a rondelle and five yellow gold pearls. On the other wire, string a rondelle and five bronze pearls. String a spacer over both wires. Repeat on the other end of the necklace.

9 String five yellow gold pearls on one wire and five bronze pearls on the other wire. String a bead ring over both wires. Repeat on the other end.

10 Repeat steps 8 and 9 until the necklace is within 2 in. of the desired length.

11 String a crimp bead over both wires. String five spacers, half the clasp, and five spacers. Go back through the crimp bead. Repeat on the other side of the necklace. Tighten the wires so that the pearls sit snugly side-by-side, check the fit, and crimp the crimp beads (Basics). Trim the excess wire. Gently close crimp covers over the crimps (Basics).

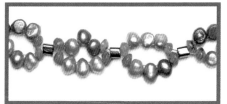

1 bracelet • Determine the finished length of your bracelet (this one is 8 in./20cm), add 5 in. (13cm), and cut two pieces of flexible beading wire to that length. On both strands, string a crimp bead, a spacer, and a clasp half. Go back through the spacer and crimp bead, tighten the wire, and crimp. String three more spacers, covering the crimp bead.

2 Separate the wires and string a rondelle, three yellow gold pearls, and a rondelle on one wire. String a rondelle, three bronze pearls, and a rondelle on the other wire. String a spacer over both wires. Repeat this pattern until the bracelet is ½ in. (1.3cm) from the desired length.

3 String three spacers, a crimp bead, a spacer, and the loop of the other clasp half. Go back through last beads strung, tighten the wires, check the fit, and crimp the crimp bead. Trim the excess wire.

materials

all projects
- chainnose pliers
- roundnose pliers
- diagonal wire cutters

necklace 16 in. (41cm)
- 30mm enamel pendant (C-Koop, 218-525-7333)
- 16-in. strand 5mm teardrop pearls in each of 2 colors, bronze and yellow gold
- 16-in. strand 4mm carnelian rondelles
- 16-in. strand 4mm cube spacer beads, bronze
- clasp (C-Koop)
- ½ in. 5.5mm cable chain
- 12 in. 24-gauge gold-filled wire
- flexible beading wire, .012–.015
- 2 crimp beads
- 2 crimp covers (optional)
- 6mm jump ring
- crimping pliers

bracelet 7½ in. (18cm)
- 5mm teardrop pearls, **18** in each of 2 colors, bronze and yellow gold
- 24 4mm carnelian rondelles
- 13 4mm cube spacer beads, bronze
- flexible beading wire, .012–.015
- 2 crimp beads
- crimping pliers

earrings
- 5mm teardrop pearls
  4 bronze
  2 yellow gold
- 10 4mm carnelian rondelles
- 6 4mm cube spacer beads, bronze
- 12 in. 24-gauge gold-filled wire
- pair earring wires

1 earrings • Cut a 6-in. (15cm) piece of wire. Center a yellow gold pearl on one wire and string a bronze pearl, a rondelle, a spacer, and a rondelle on each end.

2 Curve the wire into a loop. Bend one wire straight up and wrap the other wire around it. Trim the tail of the wrapping wire.

3 String a spacer bead and a rondelle over the wraps.

4 Make a wrapped loop above the rondelle. Open the loop on an earring wire and attach the bead unit. Make a second earring to match the first.

Metallic Gold

Gold combines with claret red to yield an elegant pair of earrings

by Anna Elizabeth Draeger

Gold draws attention to most color combinations. Here, matte-finished metallic gold beads are interspersed with deep red crystals in a rhythmic pattern, providing contrast as well as balance to the design. Notice how the gold loops emphasize the earrings' symmetry and re-creates the delicate filigree of the braided trim and the fabric's embroidery.

inspiration fabric

Create earrings with the look of fine filigree using seed beads and crystals.

editor's note

These earrings mimic a metallic trim from the home-decorating section of a fabric store. Look for other fabric trims and braids to use as inspiration for beaded jewelry.

1 Cut a 2-ft. (61cm) length of beading wire. Center three cylinder beads on the wire. Hold the ends together and string a crystal and a cylinder over both strands.

2 On one end, string a crystal, a cylinder, a crystal, and seven cylinders. Go back through the first cylinder strung in this step and pull the beads into a tight ring. Repeat with the other strand.

materials

earrings
- 44 3mm bicone crystals
- 1g Japanese cylinder beads
- flexible beading wire, .014–.015
- 2 crimp beads
- pair of earring wires
- chainnose pliers
- crimping pliers
- diagonal wire cutters

3 String a crystal on each strand and a cylinder over both strands.

4 On one strand, string a crystal, a cylinder, a crystal, and seven cylinders. Go back through the second cylinder added in step 2. String a crystal and go through the first cylinder added in this step. Repeat with the other strand.

5 Repeat step 3.

6 On one strand, string a crystal and seven cylinders. Go through the second cylinder added in step 4. String a crystal and go through the first cylinder added in this step. Repeat with the other strand.

7 Repeat step 3, then string a crystal and a crimp bead. Go back through the crimp bead, tighten the wire to create a small loop, and crimp the crimp bead (see Basics, p. 8).

8 Open the loop on an earring wire (Basics) and attach the earring. Make a second earring to match the first.

Metallic Silver

Natural and metallic materials come together in this sophisticated necklace, bracelet, and earrings set

by Helene Tsigistras

inspiration
decorative art

Brown, black, and gleaming silver merge in woven place mats that manage to look both natural and sophisticated. To achieve a similar winning effect, sparkling black crystals and silver cubes and pendants work in tandem with lustrous shell and heishi beads; this jewelry has the shine of metal and the substance of earth tones.

Three silver pendants joined by chain form the focal point of the necklace.

1 **necklace** • Cut three 3-in. (7.6cm) lengths of 24-gauge wire. String a teardrop shell on each of the wires, and make a wrapped loop above each bead (see Basics, p. 8).

2 Cut an 2-in. (5cm) length of chain. Open a jump ring (Basics), and attach a silver pendant and shell unit to the last link of the chain. Close the jump ring.

3 Open a second jump ring and attach another pendant and shell unit to the chain, four links up the chain. Use a third jump ring to attach the last pendant and shell unit to the other end of the chain.

4 Determine the finished length of your necklace (this one is 18 in./46cm), add 6 in. (15cm), and cut a strand of flexible beading wire to that length. Center the pendant unit on the strand.

5 On one side of the pendant unit, string a bicone, a spacer, a bicone, 1 in. (2.5cm) of heishi beads, a bicone, a spacer, and bicone. Repeat on the other side.

6 String a teardrop shell bead on each end of the necklace. Repeat step 5 until the necklace is within 1 in. of the desired length. You may need to adjust the number of heishi beads in the last repeat.

7 String a crimp bead, the loop of a clasp half, and a crimp bead on one end of the necklace. Go back through the crimp bead and the next few beads, tighten the wire, and crimp the crimp bead (Basics). Repeat on the other end of the necklace and trim the tails.

materials

all projects
• chainnose pliers
• roundnose pliers
• diagonal wire cutters

necklace 18 in. (46cm)
• 3 silver pendants
• 5 15mm teardrop shell beads
• 28 3mm bicone crystals, black
• 16-in. strand 4mm heishi beads, olive shell
• 14 4mm cube spacer beads, silver
• toggle clasp
• 2 in. (5cm) cable chain, 5mm
• 8 in. (20cm) 24-gauge wire
• flexible beading wire, .012–.015
• 2 crimp beads
• 3 6mm jump rings
• crimping pliers

bracelet 7½ in. (19cm)
• 3 15mm teardrop shell beads
• 55 3mm bicone crystals, black
• 16-in. strand 4mm heishi beads, olive shell
• 40 4mm cube spacer beads, silver
• two-strand clasp
• flexible beading wire, .012–.015
• 4 crimp beads
• crimping pliers

earrings
• 6 15mm teardrop shell beads
• 14 3mm bicone crystals, black
• 8 4mm heishi beads, olive shell
• 6 4mm cube spacer beads, silver
• 2 disk-shaped metal findings
• 26-in (61cm) 24-gauge wire
• pair earring wires

1 **bracelet** • Determine the finished length of your bracelet (this one is 7½ in./19cm), add 5 in. (13cm), and cut three pieces of flexible beading wire to that length. String a crimp bead and one loop of a clasp half on one wire. Tighten the wire, and crimp the crimp bead. String a crimp bead and the other loop of the clasp half on the other two wires, tighten the wires, and crimp the crimp bead.

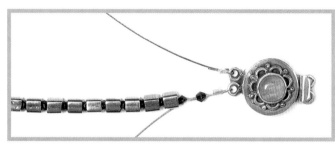

2 String a bicone over the two wires crimped together. Separate the wires. String an alternating pattern of bicones and spacers until the bracelet is within 1 in. of the desired length.

3 On the attached wire, string a bicone, 1½ in. (3.8cm) of heishi beads, a bicone, and a spacer. Repeat until the strand is within 1 in. of the desired length, ending with a bicone.

4 On the single strand, string a bicone, a spacer, a bicone, 1 in. of heishi beads, a bicone, a spacer, a bicone, and a teardrop. Repeat until the strand is within 1 in. of the desired length.

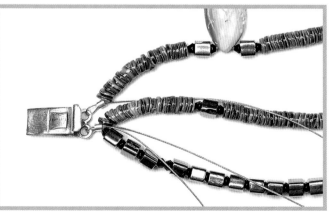

5 String a crimp bead and the corresponding loop on the other clasp half over the two strands crimped together. String a crimp bead on the teardrop strand and go through the other loop. Go back through the crimp beads, tighten the strands, and crimp the crimp beads.

1 **earrings** • Cut three 4-in. (10cm) lengths of 24-gauge wire. String one teardrop shell on each of the wires and make a set of wraps above the bead. String a bicone, a cube, and a bicone on each unit. On one unit, string three heishi beads and a bicone.

2 Make the first half of a wrapped loop on the end of each unit. Connect the longest unit to the center hole in the finding, and the shorter units to the holes on either end. Finish the wraps and trim the tails.

3 Open the loop on an earring finding and attach the disk unit. Make a second earring to match the first.

Black and White

White

inspiration nature

Whimsical charms accent a multistrand bracelet

by Anna Elizabeth Draeger

Combine black and white to make eye-catching jewelry with maximum contrast. You'll come up with something distinctive no matter what proportions you choose. Here, striped and solid-color beads mimic the zebra's mix of equal parts of black and white. Although any charms will work, I couldn't resist the chance to dangle a few zebras from my wrist.

A two-strand clasp easily accommodates a six-strand bracelet when the beads are relatively small.

materials

bracelet 7 in. (18cm)

- 16 5mm cube-shaped crystals, diagonal hole
- size 11º seed beads
  5g black with white stripe
  5g white with black stripe
  5g white
- 3 charms
- two-strand clasp
- flexible beading wire, .010–.012
- 4 crimp beads
- chainnose or crimping pliers
- diagonal wire cutters

1 Determine the finished length of your bracelet, add 5 in. (13cm), and cut six strands of beading wire to that length. String a crimp bead and one loop of the clasp over all three strands. Take all three ends back through the crimp bead and crimp it (see Basics, p. 8). Trim the tails close to the crimp. Repeat with the other three strands on the other clasp loop.

2 String a 5mm cube-shaped crystal and a black with white stripe (black) 11º seed bead on each set of strands.

3 String 20 black 11ºs on the first strand of each set of wires, string 20 white with black stripe (striped) 11ºs on the second strand, and string 20 white 11ºs on the third strand.

4 Bring the white strand from the bottom set around the black strand from the top set to link the two. String a black 11º, a crystal, and a black 11º on each set of strands.

5 String a charm on the bottom set of strands. String a crystal and a black 11º on each set of strands. Repeat steps 3–5 two more times.

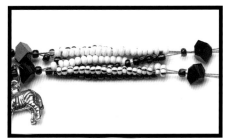

6 Repeat steps 3–4, omitting the last black 11º on each set of strands.

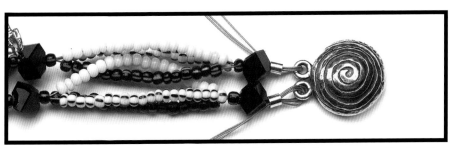

7 String a crimp bead on each set of strands. Go through the corresponding loops on the clasp and back through the crimp beads. Tighten the wires. Check the fit, and add or remove beads if necessary. Crimp the crimp beads. Trim the excess wire.

Black-and-white beads and gunmetal chain form a necklace and bracelet ensemble

by Jane Konkel

The timeless appeal of a contemporary, crackle-glazed ceramic vessel invoked the bone, wood, and heishi chosen for this necklace and bracelet set. Working with the bowl's earthy, achromatic palette results in more than a translation of color; it is also one of essence – jewelry with a primitive, handcrafted appearance, filled with significance, and reminiscent of an amulet or talisman.

Black and white

This dramatic two-part bone, wood, and gemstone necklace consists of a short strand with a single focal bead and a longer strand with multiple bead components linked with chain.

materials

both projects

- chainnose pliers
- roundnose pliers
- diagonal wire cutters
- split-ring pliers (optional)

necklace 30 in. (76cm)

- 30 x 55mm bone pendant
- 2 25 x 40mm carved bone pendants
- 3 12mm bone disks
- 4 10mm dalmatian jasper disk beads
- 3 9mm faceted round smoky quartz beads
- 8 6mm black wood beads
- 2 4mm round dalmatian jasper beads
- 2 4mm white heishi
- gunmetal lobster claw clasp
- 5 ft. (1.5m) gunmetal figaro chain, 3mm (Shipwreck Beads, 800-950-4232)
- 9 2-in. (5cm) gunmetal eye pins
- 2 6mm gunmetal split rings
- 8 4mm oval gunmetal jump rings

bracelet 6 in. (15cm) with 2½ in. (6.4cm) extender

- 2 12mm bone disks
- 3 10mm dalmatian jasper disk beads
- 9mm faceted smoky quartz beads
- 4 6mm black wood beads
- 6 4mm round dalmatian jasper beads
- gunmetal lobster claw clasp
- 1½ ft. (46cm) gunmetal figaro chain, 3mm (Shipwreck Beads)
- 6 2-in. (5cm) gunmetal eye pins
- 2 6mm gunmetal split rings
- 10 4mm oval gunmetal jump rings

1 **necklace** • On one eye pin, string a 4mm heishi, a 6mm wood bead, three bone disks, a 6mm, and a heishi. Make a plain loop (see Basics, p. 8) above the beads. On another eye pin, string a 6mm, a 25 x 40mm bone pendant, and a 6mm. Make a plain loop. Make another pendant unit on a third eye pin. On a fourth eye pin, string a 4mm round, a 6mm, four 10mm disks, a 6mm, and a 4mm round. Make a plain loop.

3 Cut two 2½-in. (6.4cm) and one 3-in. (7.6cm) pieces of chain.

4 Open the loop (Basics) of a smoky quartz dangle and attach an end link of chain. Close the loop. Repeat with the other two pieces of chain.

2 String a round smoky quartz bead on an eye pin. Make a plain loop above the bead. Make a total of three smoky quartz dangles.

5 Open a jump ring (Basics) and attach each chain to the loop on a pendant unit. Close the jump ring.

inspiration
decorative art

6 Cut two 14-in. (36cm) pieces of chain. Open a jump ring. Attach one end link of each chain and the pendant unit's remaining loop. Close the jump ring.

7 Open two jump rings and attach a bead unit to corresponding links on each chain, starting 1½ in. (3.8cm) above the connection made in step 6. Close the jump rings. Repeat with the two remaining bead units, attaching them 1 in. (2.5cm) apart on the chains.

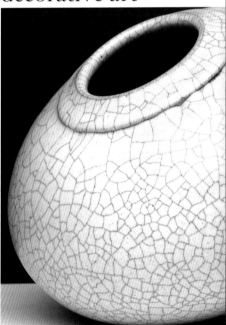

8 Cut two 7-in. (18cm) pieces of chain. Open the loop of an eye pin and attach the end link of one chain. Close the loop. Make the first half of a wrapped loop (Basics), attach one hole on the 30 x 55mm pendant, and complete the wraps. Repeat on the other edge of the pendant using the other piece of chain.

9 Check the fit. To shorten the necklace, remove an equal number of links from each of the two 14-in. chains and each of the two 7-in. chains. Working one end at a time, attach the chains' end links to a split ring. Attach the lobster claw clasp to either split ring.

1 bracelet • On each of two eye pins, string a 6mm, a 12mm disk, and a 6mm. On each of three eye pins, string a 4mm round, a 10mm disk, and a 4mm round. Make a plain loop above the end bead of each unit.

2 Cut two 5½-in. (14cm) pieces of chain. Open two jump rings and attach a bead unit to corresponding links on each chain, starting ¾ in. (1.9cm) from the end links. Close the jump rings. Repeat with the remaining bead units, attaching them 1 in. (2.5cm) apart on the chains.

3 Cut a 2-in. (5cm) piece of chain for the extender. String a round smoky quartz bead on an eye pin. Make a plain loop above the bead. Open the loop and attach an end link of the extender chain. Close the loop.

4 On each end of the bracelet, attach the chains' end links to a split ring. On one end, attach the extender to the split ring. On the other end, attach the lobster claw clasp.